Letters of

Charles Haddon Spurg

Nightingale Lane
Clapham
Feb 5

Bear . Bear . Bear .
Forbear . Forbear . Forbear

In yielding is victory
Fight the devil + love the
deacon – Love him till
he is loveable

Yours heartily
C H Spurgeon

Letters of
Charles Haddon Spurgeon

Selected with Notes by
Iain H. Murray

THE BANNER OF TRUTH TRUST

THE BANNER OF TRUTH TRUST
3 Murrayfield Road, Edinburgh EH12 6EL
P.O. Box 621, Carlisle, Pennsylvania 17013, U.S.A.

© Banner of Truth Trust 1992
First published 1992
ISBN 0 85151 606 8

Typeset in 10½/12pt Linotron Bembo
at The Spartan Press Ltd, Lymington, Hants
and printed in Great Britain by
BPCC Hazells Ltd
Member of BPCC Ltd

CONTENTS

10 ILLNESS AND LETTERS FROM MENTON 161

11 THE DOWN-GRADE CONTROVERSY 177

INTRODUCTION

It is a happy thing that this selection of Spurgeon's Letters should be appearing at the time of the centenary of his death. In the hundred years since January 31, 1892 the only such collection previously published was *The Letters of Charles Haddon Spurgeon*, edited by Charles Spurgeon, in 1923. That volume has been long out of print and while its republication would have been worthwhile there was a major reason for the present publishers to prefer a new selection. Thirty-one years after his father's death, Charles Spurgeon was still restricted in his choice of correspondence by the fact that 'in a very large number of instances the epistles are of such a private nature that it would be a breach of confidence, as well as of courtesy, to make them public.'[1] No such consideration need operate today and it is therefore possible to include in this book a large number of letters not previously published.

I am indebted to my friends John J. Murray and Michael Boland for sharing – some years ago now – in the research necessary for this new selection. The archives of Spurgeon's College at West Norwood, London, were indispensable to us in this labour. Copies of many Spurgeon letters have been gathered at the College since Charles Spurgeon completed his work in 1923 and the Christian world will be grateful to the Principal and the College authorities for making these available for publication.

---

[1] *The Letters of Charles Haddon Spurgeon*, Marshall Brothers, London, 1923, p.7.

While this selection only partially follows a chrono-
logical order, and a number of major events in his life are
not covered at all, it will be found to provide an
introduction to his life which is uniquely valuable. 'A
man's private letters often let you into the secrets of the
heart,' Spurgeon once wrote and this was eminently true
in his own case. If these pages are far from containing all
that can be said about the preacher, they certainly reveal
the real man and they do so in a way which leaves us
feeling that we have joined his circle of intimate friends.

The preparation of these pages has constantly impres-
sed a number of Spurgeon's characteristics upon us, none
more so than the industry which enabled him to
accomplish so much in fifty-seven years. He maintained
such a large correspondence that letter writing might
have been his sole occupation. 'I am immersed to the chin
in letters', he wrote to his friend William Williams in
1885. His son Charles records, 'He often said, "I am only
a poor clerk, driving the pen hour after hour; here is
another whole morning gone, and nothing done but
letters! letters! letters!"' Spurgeon's letters went to all
parts of the world but they were also necessary to people
within his own congregation in the age before the
telephone. One of Spurgeon's elders alone preserved
some eighty letters from him.

Attending to correspondence was, of course, far from
being Spurgeon's main occupation. There were three
sermons to prepare weekly for his Metropolitan
Tabernacle congregation (which numbered 5,311
members at the time of his death). There were some 300
Sunday School teachers, with 8,000 scholars, to super-
vise. He had also to preside over a Pastors' College and a
children's Orphanage, in addition to preparing a
monthly magazine, *The Sword and the Trowel*, and other
works of authorship.

But letter writing remained at the heart of Spurgeon's ministry and only hard work, along with a God-given devotion to people, can explain how he sustained such an output. Occasionally he gave hints in *The Sword and the Trowel* that his burden of correspondence might be lessened by a little more consideration. For example, when it was known that he was going north to Scotland for a much needed holiday in the summer of 1878, he was beset with invitations to stop here and there for 'two hours' to preach. In *The Sword and the Trowel*, for August of that year, he commented (with his usual touch of humour), 'How many pence we have been fined in the form of postage for replies to these insanely kind demands we will not calculate, but it is rather too absurd!' Despite this kind of thing, Spurgeon never handed over the work of replying to letters to secretaries. Anything of importance – interpreted generously – had his attention and obtained a personal response in his own clear, copper-plate hand, written, generally, in his favourite violet ink. He rarely seems to have dictated letters and when he sometimes made use of standard lithographed acknowledgements for gifts received for the Orphanage, or other institutions, he commonly would write some additional lines in his own hand.

While the sheer weight and size of Spurgeon's words was known to the few close friends in whom he would confide (such as William Williams, quoted above), the letters themselves reveal little of it. He never parades his busyness and the spirit of his correspondence confirms the observation of Williams that 'his normal stock was rather one of calm delightful *restfulness*'.

The letters now published in this book for the first time reveal aspects of Spurgeon that were kept to a large degree from public view in his lifetime – these include his supervision of detail in the work of the Metropolitan

Tabernacle and the College; his pain and, sometimes, depression, over the drift from orthodox Christianity (culminating in the Down-Grade controversy); and the extent of the physical illness which was so repeatedly present in the last twenty and more years of his life. 'How much he suffered', writes G. H. Pike, 'no mortal knew save himself.' The following pages will bring these things into clearer view and while they confirm words he once spoke, 'You may write my life across the sky; I have nothing to conceal', they, more importantly, set forth the grace of the God who sustained him and made him all that he was.

Spurgeon, says William Williams, expected no permanency for his letters for the good reason that though 'there is not better ink than that to be bought in penny bottles', he did not think it would be durable. Thankfully, not only have many of the original letters survived, but through the work of Charles Spurgeon and those who have laboured in collecting the archives at Spurgeon's College, the ministry of his correspondence can continue today. Never was there greater need of Christians 'true as steel to the old faith' and this selection is sent out with the belief that it will serve to encourage such men and women across the world.

Iain H. Murray
3 Murrayfield Road
Edinburgh
July, 1991

BIOGRAPHICAL NOTES

1834	June 19	Born at Kelvedon, Essex
1850	January 6	Converted at Colchester
1851	October	Becomes pastor of Waterbeach Baptist Chapel, Cambridge
1854	April	Called to New Park Street Chapel, Southwark
1855	January	Publication of weekly sermon begins
1856	January 8	Marries Susannah Thompson
1861	March 18	Metropolitan Tabernacle opened
1865	January	Publication of *The Sword and the Trowel* begins
1891	June 7	Last sermon at Tabernacle
1892	January 31	Dies at Menton

1: FIRST YEARS AS A CHRISTIAN

1850 – 1853

[The Rev John Spurgeon, 1810–1902]

Newmarket
January 30, 1850

My dear Father,[1]

I am most happy and comfortable, I could not be more so whilst sojourning on earth, 'like a pilgrim or a stranger, as all my fathers were.' There are but four boarders, and about twelve day-boys. I have a nice little mathematical class, and have quite as much time for study as I had before. I can get good religious conversations with Mr Swindell, which is what I most need. Oh, how unprofitable has my past life been! Oh, that I should have been so long time blind to those celestial wonders, which now I can in a measure behold! Who can refrain from speaking of the marvellous love of Jesus which, I hope, has opened mine eyes![2] Now I see Him, I can firmly trust to Him for my eternal salvation. Yet soon I doubt again; then I am sorrowful; again faith appears, and I become confident of my interest in Him. I feel now as if I could do everything, and give up everything for Christ, and then I know it would be nothing in comparison with His love. I am hopeless of ever making anything like a return. How sweet is prayer! I would be always engaged in it. How

[1] In August of the previous year Spurgeon, aged fifteen, had left his home in Colchester to be an 'under tutor' at the academy of a Mr Swindell at Newmarket. In this service he was also expected to continue his own education.

[2] After a lengthy period under conviction Spurgeon's conversion had occurred this same month on January 6.

beautiful is the Bible! I never loved it so before; it seems to me as necessary food. I feel that I have not one particle of spiritual life in me but what the Spirit placed there. I feel that I cannot live if He depart; I tremble and fear lest I should grieve Him. I dread lest sloth or pride should overcome me, and I should dishonour the gospel by neglect of prayer, or the Scriptures, or by sinning against God. Truly, that will be a happy place where we shall get rid of sin and this depraved corrupt nature. When I look at the horrible pit and the hole from which I have been digged, I tremble lest I should fall into it, and yet rejoice that I am on the King's highway. I hope you will forgive me for taking up so much space about myself; but at present my thoughts are most about it.

From the Scriptures, is it not apparent that, immediately upon receiving the Lord Jesus, it is a part of duty openly to profess Him? I firmly believe and consider that baptism is the command of Christ, and shall not feel quite comfortable if I do not receive it. I am unworthy of such things, but so am I unworthy of Jesu's love. I hope I have received the blessing of the one and think I ought to take the other also.

My very best love to you and my dear Mother; I seem to love you more than ever, because you love my Lord Jesus. I hope yourself, dear Mother, Archer, Eliza, Emily, Louisa, and Lottie,[1] are well; love to all . . .

May we all, after this fighting life is over, meet in –

> *That Kingdom of immense delight,*
> *Where health, and peace, and joy unite,*
> *Where undeclining pleasures rise,*
> *And every wish hath full supplies;*

[1] His brother, James Archer, born 1837, and sisters, Eliza, Emily, Louisa and Charlotte, born 1836, 1839, 1845 and 1846 respectively.

and while you are here, may the blessings of the gospel abound toward you, and may we as a family be all devoted to the Lord! May all blessings be upon us, and may –

> I ever remain,
> Your dutiful and affectionate son,
> CHAS. H. SPURGEON

[*Mrs Eliza Spurgeon, 1815–1883*]

Newmarket
Feb. 19, 1850

My dear Mother,

I hope the long space between my letters will be excused, as I assure you I am fully occupied. I read French exercises every night with Mr Swindell, – Monsr. Perret comes once every week for an hour. I have 33 houses at present where I leave tracts, – I happened to take a district formerly supplied by Mrs Andrews, who last lived in this house, and Miss Anna Swindell. Next Wednesday, – I mean to-morrow, – I am to go to a meeting of the tract-distributors. They have been at a stand-still, and hope now to start afresh. On Thursday, Mr Simpson intends coming to talk with me upon the most important of all subjects. Oh, how I wish that I could do something for Christ! Tract distribution is so pleasant and easy that it is nothing, – nothing in itself, much less when it is compared with the amazing debt of gratitude I owe.

I have written to grandfather,[1] and have received a very nice letter. I have been in the miry Slough of Despond; he sends me a strong consolation, but is that

---

[1] Rev James Spurgeon of Stambourne.

what I want? Ought I not rather to be reproved for my deadness and coldness? I pray as if I did not pray, hear as if I did not hear, and read as if I did not read – such is my deadness and coldness. I had a glorious revival on Saturday and Sunday. When I can do anything, I am not quite so dead. Oh, what a horrid state! It seems as if no real child of God could ever look so coldly on, and think so little of, the love of Jesus and His glorious atonement. Why is not my heart always warm? Is it not because of my own sins? I fear lest this deadness be but the prelude to death, – spiritual death. I have still a sense of my own weakness, nothingness, and utter inability to do any-thing in and of myself, – I pray God that I may never lose it, – I am sure I must if left to myself, and then, when I am cut off from Him, in Whom my great strength lieth, I shall be taken by the Philistines in my own wicked heart, and have mine eyes for ever closed to all spiritual good. Pray for me, O my dear Father and Mother! Oh, that Jesus would pray for me! Then I shall be delivered, and everlastingly saved. I should like to be always reading my Bible, and be daily gaining greater insight into it by the help of the Spirit. I can get but very little time, as Mr S. pushes me on in Greek and French.

I have come to a resolution that, by God's help, I will profess the name of Jesus as soon as possible if I may be admitted into His Church on earth. It is an honour, – no difficulty, – grandfather encourages me to do so, and I hope to do so both as a duty and privilege. I trust that I shall then feel that the bonds of the Lord are upon me, and have a more powerful sense of my duty to walk circumspectly. Conscience has convinced me that it is a duty to be buried with Christ in baptism, although I am sure it constitutes no part of salvation. I am very glad that you have no objection to my doing so. Mr Swindell is a Baptist.

You must have been terribly frightened when the chimney fell down; what a mercy that none were hurt! There was a great deal of damage here from the wind. My cold is about the same as it was at home, it has been worse. I take all the care I can; I suppose it will go away soon. How are all the little ones? Give my love to them, and to Archer and Eliza. How does Archer get on? Accept my best love for yourself and Father. I hope you are well,

> And remain,
> Your affectionate son,
> CHARLES HADDON SPURGEON

[*The Rev John Spurgeon*]

Newmarket
April 6, 1850

My dear Father,

You will be pleased to hear that, last Thursday night, I was admitted as a member.[1] Oh, that I may henceforth live more for the glory of Him, by Whom I feel assured that I shall be everlastingly saved! Owing to my scruples on account of baptism, I did not sit down at the Lord's table, and cannot in conscience do so until I am baptised. To one who does not see the necessity of baptism, it is perfectly right and proper to partake of this blessed privilege; but were I to do so, I conceive would be to tumble over the wall, since I feel persuaded it is Christ's appointed way of professing Him. I am sure this is the only view which I have of baptism. I detest the idea that I

---

[1] i.e., of the Congregational church at Newmarket.

can do a single thing towards my own salvation. I trust that I feel sufficiently the corruption of my own heart to know that, instead of doing one iota to forward my own salvation, my old corrupt heart would impede it, were it not that my Redeemer is mighty, and works as He pleases.

Since last Thursday I have been unwell in body, but I may say that my soul has been almost in Heaven. I have been able to see my title clear, and to know and believe that, sooner than one of God's little ones shall perish, God Himself will cease to be, Satan will conquer the King of kings, and Jesus will no longer be the Saviour of the elect. Doubts and fears may soon assail me, but I will not dread to meet them if my Father has so ordained it; He knows best. Were I never to have another visit of grace, and be always doubting from now until the day of my death, yet 'the foundation of the Lord standeth sure, having this seal, the Lord knoweth them that are His.' I see now the secret, how it is that you were enabled to bear up under all your late trials. This faith is far more than any of us deserve; all beyond hell is mercy, but this is a mighty one. Were it not all of sovereign, electing, almighty grace, I, for one, could never hope to be saved. God says, 'You shall,' and not all the devils in hell, let loose upon a real Christian, can stop the workings of God's sovereign grace, for in due time the Christian cries, 'I will.' Oh, how little love have I for One Who has thus promised to save me by so great a salvation, and Who will certainly perform His promise!

I trust that the Lord is working among my tract people, and blessing my little effort. I have most interesting and encouraging conversation with many of them. Oh, that I could see but one sinner constrained to come to Jesus! How I long for the time when it may please God to make me, like you, my Father, a successful preacher of the gospel! I almost envy you your exalted privilege. May the dew of Hermon and the increase of the Spirit rest upon your labours! Your unworthy son tries to pray for you and his Mother, that grace and peace may be with you. Oh, that the God of mercy would incline Archer's heart to Him, and make him a partaker of His grace! Ask him if he will believe me when I say that one drop of the pleasure of religion is worth ten thousand oceans of the pleasures of the unconverted, and then ask him if he is not willing to prove the fact by experience. Give my love to my dear Mother . . .

As Mr Cantlow's baptising season will come round this month, I have humbly to beg your consent, as I will not act against your will, and should very much like to commune next month.[1] I have no doubt of your permission. We are all one in Christ Jesus; forms and ceremonies, I trust, will not make us divided . . .

With my best love and hopes that you are all well,

> I remain,
> Your affectionate son,
> Not only as to the flesh, but in the faith,
> CHARLES HADDON SPURGEON

[*Mrs Eliza Spurgeon*]

Newmarket
May 1, 1850

My dear Mother,

Many very happy returns of your Birthday! In this instance, my wish will certainly be realised, for in

---

[1] W. W. Cantlow at Isleham was the nearest Baptist pastor to Newmarket. The permission of his parents (who were Congregationalists) being given, Spurgeon was baptised at Isleham Ferry, on the River Lark, May 3, 1850.

Heaven you are sure to have an eternity of happy days. May you, in your coming years, live beneath the sweet smiles of the God of peace; may joy and singing attend your footsteps to a blissful haven of rest and tranquillity! Your birthday will now be doubly memorable, for on the third of May, the boy for whom you have so often prayed, the boy of hopes and fears, your first-born, will join the visible Church of the redeemed on earth, and will bind himself doubly to the Lord his God, by open profession. You, my Mother, have been the great means in God's hand of rendering me what I hope I am. Your kind, warning Sabbath–evening addresses were too deeply settled on my heart to be forgotten. You, by God's blessing, prepared the way for the preached Word, and for that holy book, *The Rise and Progress*.[1] If I have any courage, if I feel prepared to follow my Saviour, not only into the water, but should He call me, even into the fire, I love you as the preacher to my heart of such courage, as my praying, watching Mother. Impossible, I think it is, that I should ever cease to love you, or you to love me, yet not nearly so impossible as that the Lord our Father should cease to love either of us, be we ever so doubtful of it, or ever so disobedient. I hope you may one day have cause to rejoice, should you see me, the unworthy instrument of God, preaching to others, – yet have I vowed in the strength of my only Strength, in the name of my Beloved, to devote myself for ever to His cause. Do you not think it would be a bad beginning were I, knowing it to be my duty to be baptised, to shrink from it? If you are now as happy as I am, I can wish no more than that you may continue so. I am the happiest creature, I think, upon this globe.

---

[1] *Rise and Progress of Religion in the Soul*, Philip Doddridge. See *Early Years*, p.86.

I hope you have enjoyed your visit, and that it will help much to establish your health. I dare not ask you to write, for I know you are always so busy that it is quite a task to you. I hope my letter did not pain you, dear Mother; my best love to you, be assured that I would not do anything to grieve you, and I am sure that I remain,

Your affectionate son,
CHARLES HADDON

Mr and Mrs Swindell's respects to you and dear Father.

[*Mrs Eliza Spurgeon*]

Newmarket
June 11, 1850

My dear Mother,

Many thanks to you for your valuable letter. Your notes are so few and far between, and are such a trouble to you, that one now and then is quite a treasure . . .

I have had two opportunities of addressing the Sunday-school children, and have endeavoured to do so as a dying being to dying beings. I am bound to Newmarket by holy bonds. I have 70 people whom I regularly visit on Saturday. I do not give a tract, and go away; but I sit down, and endeavour to draw their attention to spiritual realities. I have great reason to believe the Lord is working, – the people are so kind, and so pleased to see me. I cannot bear to leave them. We are so feeble here that the weakest cannot be spared. We have a pretty good attendance at prayer-meetings; but so few praying men, that I am constantly called upon . . .

One of our Deacons, Mr —, is constantly inviting me to his house, he is rather an Arminian;[1] but so are the majority of Newmarket Christians. Grandfather has written to me; he does not blame me for being a Baptist, but hopes I shall not be one of the tight-laced, strict-communion sort. In that, we are agreed. I certainly think we ought to forget such things in others when we come to the Lord's table. I can, and hope I shall be charitable to unbaptised Christians, though I think they are mistaken. It is not a great matter; men will differ; we ought both to follow our own consciences, and let others do the same. I think the time would be better spent in talking upon vital godliness than in disputing about forms. I trust the Lord is weaning me daily from all self-dependence, and teaching me to look at myself as less than nothing. I know that I am perfectly dead without Him; it is His work; I am confident that He will accomplish it, and that I shall see the face of my Beloved in His own house in glory.

My enemies are many, and they hate me with cruel hatred, yet with Jehovah Jesus on my side, why should I fear? I will march on in His almighty strength to certain conquest and victory. I am so glad that Sarah, too, is called, that two of us in one household at one time should thus openly profess the Saviour's name. We are brother and sister in the Lord; may our Father often give each of us the refreshing visits of His grace! I feel as if I could say with Paul, 'Would that I were even accursed, so that my brethren according to the flesh might be saved!' What a joy if God should prove that they are redeemed ones included in the covenant of grace! I long to see your face, and let my heart beat with yours, whilst we talk of the glorious things pertaining to eternal life. My best love to

[1]For Spurgeon's understanding of Arminianism see *The Forgotten Spurgeon*, Iain H. Murray, Banner of Truth Trust, 1966.

you and Father, may the Angel of the covenant dwell with you, and enchant you by the visions of His grace! Love to Eliza, Archer (many happy returns to him), Emily, Lottie, and Louisa; may they become members of the church in our house! I am very glad you are so well. I am so, but hard at work for the Examination, so allow me to remain,

Your most affectionate son,
CHARLES

Master H— shall be attended to; be ye always ready for every good work. I have no time, but it shall be done.

[*The Rev John Spurgeon*]

[9 Union Road]
Cambridge
19th Sept., '50

My dear Father,

I received your kind letter in due time. I joined the Church here at the Lord's table last Ordinance day.[1] I shall write for my dismission; I intended to have done so before. The Baptists are by far the most respectable denomination in Cambridge;[2] there are three Baptist Chapels, – St Andrew's Street, where we attend, Zion Chapel, and Eden Chapel. There is a very fine Wesleyan Chapel and some others. I teach in the Sunday-school all the afternoon. Mr Leeding takes the morning work. Last

[1] At the instigation of his father, Spurgeon had recently moved to the school of Charles Leeding in Cambridge where he was again both a tutor and student.
[2] He is referring, of course, to Nonconformist denominations.

Sabbath-day we had a funeral sermon from Hebrews vi. 11, 12. We have a prayer-meeting at 7 in the morning, and one after the evening service; they are precious means of grace, I trust, to my soul. How soon would the lamps go out did not our mighty Lord supply fresh oil; and if it were not for His unshaken promise to supply our need out of the fulness of His grace, poor indeed should we be.

Yes, where Jesus comes, He comes to reign; how I wish He would reign more in my heart; then I might hope that every atom of self, self-confidence, and self-righteousness, would be swept out of my soul. I am sure I long for the time when all evil affections, corrupt desires, and rebellious, doubting thoughts shall be overcome, and completely crushed beneath the Prince's feet, and my whole soul be made pure and holy. But so long as I am encaged within this house of clay, I know they will lurk about, and I must have hard fighting though the victory by grace is sure. Praying is the best fighting; nothing else will keep them down.

I have written a letter to grandfather; I am sorry he is so poorly. He wants the promises now, and why may not young and old live upon them? They are the bread-corn of Heaven, the meat of the Kingdom; and who that has once tasted them will turn to eat husks without any sweetness and comfort in them? God's power will keep all His children; while He says to them, 'How shall ye who are dead to sin live any longer therein?' I feel persuaded that I shall never fathom the depths of my own natural depravity, nor climb to the tops of the mountains of God's eternal love. I feel constrained day by day to fall flat down upon the promises, and leave my soul in Jesu's keeping. It is He that makes my feet move even in the slow obedience which marks them at present, and every attainment of grace must come from Him. I would go forth by prayer, like the Israelites, to gather up this Heavenly manna, and live upon free-grace.

Add to all your great kindness and love to me, through my life, a constant remembrance of me in your prayers. I thank you for those petitions which you and dear Mother have so often sent up to the mercy-seat for me. Give my love to my sisters and brother, and accept the same for yourself and dear Mother. Hoping you are all quite well.

> I remain,
> Your obedient, affectionate son,
> CHAS. H. SPURGEON

[*Mrs Walker*]

> Cambridge
> June 3, 1851

My dear Aunt,

I have just received a note from dear father with your address, and feeling some little sorrow for past negligence, I have not put off writing to you.

I make my old complaint again, – I have nothing to write about . . . I hope to see the Exhibition with father and mother. I say, it will be quite a treat to see them there. We have our Missionary meeting next Sabbath. Last Sunday we had old Mr Jay of Bath; a real wonder he is. The place was crammed everywhere. He is eighty three or eighty four, I think.[1]

I do not know anything of my future steps. I have nothing to do with it; I have no wish but to remain here,

[1]See *The Autobiography of William Jay* (1769–1853), edited by George Redford and John Angell James, reprinted Banner of Truth Trust, 1974 and currently still in print.

but am perfectly contented to do as friends think best. I trust I have endeavoured to improve my mind – others will best judge with what success. If I can earn my own living and manage to progress, all my wishes are attained. I have pursued Divinity with some ardour, and only wish that I could learn more of its wondrous mysteries, and feel more deeply the effects of its doctrines. In this course I find fresh and ever increasing delight. May I never go astray or leave the path the Bible prescribes.

It is a mercy Uncle is so well. You have had a rough year; you have been tried severely. No doubt you will derive benefit from it. Accept my best love and thanks, for whenever I write I must thank you for past kindnesses, but thanks are no returns.

Your affectionate nephew,
C. H. SPURGEON

[*Mrs Walker*]

Colchester
June 25, 1851

My dear Aunt,

I enclose this in Uncle's note. Is he better? I have much enjoyed my three days in London, and am now happy at home. I am very thankful that, if spared, I am going back to Cambridge. Of my progress there, I am not ashamed; it should and might have been greater, but still it is somewhat. My faults I have not learned there; I had the same at Maidstone, and I am not at all fond of having blame thrown on the place where Providence has placed me. I am all fault, but what God's grace has made right. I am content to be evil spoken of, if I can but grow in grace and serve God. Where I have most opportunity of telling sinners the way of salvation, and of preparation for a future course of labour, I trust I shall always feel most happy. Human wisdom I desire to gain, but only in subservience, and as handmaid to spiritual knowledge and Divine instruction.

Grandfather is with us now; he preached last night on 'Cast thy burden upon the Lord, and He shall sustain thee: He shall never suffer the righteous to be moved.' A blessed thing it must be for the new-born sons of God to have such a stay in the hour of trouble; and he who having left his own righteousness, trusts alone on Jesus, has a perfect right to this promise.

Mother is gone to old Mr Merchant's 51st Anniversary at Layer Breton. He is almost past preaching, and stands a monument of the unchanging love of God, who, having once loved a person, will always love him. The motto over his pulpit is, 'We preach Christ, and Him crucified.' I am sure you need all the comforts of the gospel now, and I wish I knew enough to be able to give them faithfully and successfully; that is reserved for future lessons of experience. None who rely on Jesus Christ will ever find their troubles too heavy; for all those who take Him as their whole Saviour, He is a supporter. May God deal kindly with you, and support you!

Love to self and Uncle from all.

> I am,
> Your affectionate nephew,
> C. H. SPURGEON

[*The Rev John Spurgeon*]

Cambridge
October 15, 1851

My dear Father,

I received your most welcome note, and beg pardon if you think me negligent in returning thanks. I have been busily employed every Lord's day; not at home once yet, nor do I expect to be this year. Last Sunday, I went to a place called Waterbeach, where there is an old-established Church, but not able to support a minister.[1] I have engaged to supply to the end of the month. They had, for twenty years, a minister who went over from Cambridge in the same way as you go to Tollesbury. After that, they tried to have a minister; but as they could not keep him, he has left, and they will have to do as they used to do. There is rail there and back, and it is only six miles.

I am glad you have such good congregations. I feel no doubt there is a great work doing there; – the fields are ripe unto the harvest, the seed you have sown has yielded plenty of green, let us hope there will be abundance of wheat. Give my love to dear Mother; you have indeed had trials. I always like to see how you bear them. I think I shall never forget that time when Mother and all were so ill. How you were supported! How cheerful you were! You said, in a letter to me, –

> *When troubles, like a gloomy cloud,*
> *Have gathered thick, and thundered loud,*
> *He near my side has always stood;*
> *His loving kindness, O how good!*

[1]This proved to be the beginning of Spurgeon's first (part-time) pastorate. After preaching a first sermon in a cottage of Teversham, near Cambridge, when he was still fifteen, Spurgeon had quickly become a member of the Cambridge Lay Preachers' Association. Waterbeach was one of the thirteen villages served by the Association.

I trust that you are all well, and that the clouds are blown away. I am quite well, I am happy to say. Where is Aunt? It is four months since I have heard anything from her, or about her. We have no settled minister yet, nor do we expect any. I thank you much for your sermon; it will just do for me.

How greatly must I admire the love that could choose me to speak the gospel, and to be the happy recipient of it! I trust my greatest concern is to grow in grace, and to go onward in the blessed course. I feel jealous lest my motive should change, fearing lest I should be my own servant instead of the Lord's. How soon may we turn aside without knowing it, and begin to seek objects below the sacred office!

Mr and Mrs L. are well, and send their respects. Grandfather has asked me to go to Stambourne, but I cannot afford to go his way. With love to you, dear Father, and all at home,

> I am,
> Your affectionate son,
> CHAS. H. SPURGEON

> Cambridge
> Feb. 24, 1852

My dear Father,

Mr Angus, the tutor of Stepney College, [London], preached for us on Sunday, Feb. 1. Being at my own place, I had no opportunity of seeing him, and was very surprised, when, on Monday, I was told that he wanted to see me. I assure you, I never mentioned myself to him, nor to anyone – this came quite unexpectedly. I suppose the deacons of our church, hearing of my doings at Waterbeach, had thought right to mention me to him.

Well, I went to the place of meeting; but, by a very singular occurrence, we missed each other; he waited in the parlour, while I was shown into the drawing-room, and the servant forgot to tell him I had come. As he was going to London, and could not wait, he wrote the enclosed.

I have waited thus long because (1) I wanted to get a little more to tell you; (2) I do not want to appear to desire to go to College at your expense. I do not wish to go until I can pay for it with my own money, or until friends offer to help, because I do not want to burden you. It is said by almost all friends that I ought to go to College. I have no very great desire for it; in fact, none at all. Yet I have made it a matter of prayer, and I trust, yea, I am confident, God will guide me.

Of course, you are my only earthly director and guide in these matters; your judgment always has been best; you must know best. But perhaps you will allow me just to state my own opinion, not because I shall trust in it, but only that you may see my inclination. I think, then, (with all deference to you,) that I had better not go to College *yet*, at least not just now, for –

1. Whatever advantages are to be derived from such a course of study, I shall be more able to improve when my powers are more developed than they are at present. When I know more, I shall be more able to learn.

2. Providence has thrown me into a great sphere of usefulness, – a congregation of often 450, a loving and praying church, and an awakened audience. Many already own that the preaching has been with power from Heaven. Now, ought I to leave them?

3. In a few years' time, I hope to improve my financial position so as to be at no expense to you, or at least not

for all. I should not like to know that you were burdening yourself for me. I should love to work my own way as much as possible. I know you like this feeling.

4. I am not uneducated. I have many opportunities of improvement now; all I want is more time; but even that, Mr Leeding would give me, if it were so arranged. I have plenty of practice; and do we not learn to preach by preaching? You know what my style is. I fancy it is not very College-like. Let it be never so bad, God has blessed it, and I believe He will yet more. All I do right, He does in me, and the might is of Him. I am now well off; I think as well off as anyone of my age, and I am sure quite as happy. If I were in need I think the people might be able to raise more for me. Now, shall I throw myself out, and trust to Providence as to whether I shall ever get another place as soon as I leave College?

5. But, no; – I have said enough, – you are to judge, not I. I leave it to God and yourself, but, still, I should like you to decide in this way. Of course, I have a will, and you now know it; but I say 'Not mine, but your will, and God's will.'

I have just acknowledged the letter, and said that I could make no reply until I had consulted my friends. I think it might be as well, if you think so, too, to let Mr Angus know as much as is right of my present position, that he may be favourable toward me at any future time . . .

I hope you will excuse my scrawl, for, believe me, I am fully employed. Last night, I thought of writing; but was called out to see a dying man, and I thought I dare not refuse. The people at W— would not like to get even a hint of my leaving them. I do not know why they love me, but they do; it is the Lord's doing.

Give my love, and many thanks to dear Mother, Archer, and sisters. If at any time you think a letter from me would be useful, just hint as much, and I will write one.

May God keep me, in every place, from every evil, and dwell with you, and abide with you for ever, and with my best love,

> I am,
> Dear Father,
> Your affectionate son,
> CHARLES

[*The Rev Richard Knill*[1]]

Cambridge
Feb. 7, '53

My dear Sir,

I feel confident that you will pardon the liberty I take when you read the occasion of it. I have for some time wished to write to you, but could not find you out, until in *The Banner* I observed a notice of your preaching in the theatre of Chester.

Eight or nine years ago, you were travelling, as a Deputation from the London Missionary Society, in the county of Essex. Among other places, you preached at the village of Stambourne. I was then a little boy staying at my grandfather's (Rev. Jas. Spurgeon). You kindly noticed me; I read at family prayer; you took me by your side, and talked to me in a very affectionate manner. You told me a tale of a little boy in Colchester; we went into an arbour in the garden, there you asked me to sing, and I joined in as well as I could. I shall never forget the way in which you tried to lead me to the Saviour. Your

---

[1]For further comment on the remarkable story in this letter see *C. H. Spurgeon, The Early Years, 1834–1859*, Banner of Truth Trust, 1962, pp. 27–28.

conversation and spirit were all a father's could have been, and that one interview has made my heart yours. My eyes rejoice to see your name, and the mention of it brings up emotions of gratitude. In fact, unknown to you, a few words you then spoke have been a sort of star to my existence, and my friends look on them with half the reverence of prophecy. You meant them not perhaps to last so long, but now they are imperishable; they were to this effect, and were heard by more than one: 'I think this little man will one day be a preacher of the gospel, and I hope a successful one. I think you will preach in Rowland Hill's Chapel; and when you do, tell the people this verse, "God moves in a mysterious way, etc.' You told me to learn the hymn, and said it seemed perhaps unlikely, but Providence had wrought wonders, and you thought it would be so. This is often mentioned by my grandfather; and somehow, though I am far enough from being superstitious, it holds me fast, and I do confidently, and yet, somehow (and paradoxically), distrustfully, look forward to the time when the whole shall come to pass.

When sixteen and a half years old, I was persuaded to preach in the villages, having for some time been often called to address children in Sabbath Schools, and always gaining attention, perhaps from my youth as much as anything. Once started in lay-preaching around Cambridge – where I was and am still assistant in a school, – I put my soul into the work. Having been invited to supply, for one Sabbath, the Baptist Church at Waterbeach, I did so; I was invited to continue, and have now been the minister of the congregation for one year and four months. The chapel is always full, many profess to have felt the power of Divine grace, and residents in the neighbourhood say that there is a visible reform manifest; God has used things that are not, to bring to nought things that are. I preach thrice on the Sabbath; and often, indeed, almost constantly, five times in the week-nights. My salary being insufficient, I still remain in the school. Though the congregation is large, they being poor, or men of small property, are unable to do much, – though their kindness may be judged of from the fact that I have been to sixty-two different houses to dine on the Lord's Day. Thus are your words in part realised.

Though I do not say that your conversation did then lead to my conversion, yet the thought of what I conceived might be my position one day ever worked in me a desire to gain true religion, which even then I knew was the great essential in a minister. I long for nothing more earnestly than to serve God with all my might. My education is amply sufficient for my present station, and I have means and desires for further improvement.

The particulars I have given are perhaps too lengthy, but you will excuse it. I could not refrain from letting you know what is no doubt more interesting to me than to you. I pray that, while standing on the polluted ground, (in Chester theatre), you may consecrate it in many a heart by being the means of their conversion. Your words spoken in season have been good to me; and if I am of any use in the army of the living God, I owe it in great part to you that I ever enlisted in it. I am not nineteen yet; and need, and trust I shall have, a mention in your prayers.

> With the greatest respect,
> I am,
> Yours truly,
> CHARLES SPURGEON

P.S. Since you are much engaged, I shall scarcely expect a line from you; but if I should be happy enough to receive one, I shall be rejoiced.

Cambridge
December —, 1853

My dear Father,

I concluded rather abruptly before; – but you are often called out from your writing, and therefore can excuse it in me. I hardly know what I left unsaid. I hope to be at home three days. I think of running down from London on Tuesday, January 3rd, and to go home by Bury on Friday, 6th. I hope it will be a sweet visit though a short one.

Should I be settled in London,[1] I will come and see you often. I do not anticipate going there with much pleasure. I am contented where I am; but if God has more for me to do, then let me go and trust in Him. The London people are rather higher in Calvinism than I am; but I have succeeded in bringing one church to my own views, and will trust, with Divine assistance, to do the same with another. I am a Calvinist; I love what someone called 'glorious Calvinism', but 'Hyperism' is too hot-spiced for my palate.

I found a relation in London; a daughter of Thomas Spurgeon, at Ballingdon. On the Monday, she came and brought the unmarried sister, who you will remember was at home when we called last Christmas. I shall have no objection to preach for Mr Langford on Wednesday, January 4th, if he wishes it.

I spent the Monday in going about London, climbed to the top of St Paul's, and left some money with the booksellers.

My people are very sad; some wept bitterly at the sight of me, although I made no allusion to the subject in the

---

[1]This letter was clearly written after Spurgeon had fulfilled an invitation to preach at New Park Street Chapel, Southwark, London, on December 11, 1853. He was called to this, his life-long pastorate, the following month.

pulpit, as it is too uncertain to speak of publicly. It is Calvinism they want in London, and any Arminian preaching will not be endured. Several in the church are far before me in theological acumen; they would not admit that it is so; but they all expressed their belief that my originality, or even eccentricity, was the very thing to draw a London audience. The chapel is one of the finest in the denomination; somewhat in the style of our Cambridge Museum. A Merry Christmas to you all; a Happy New Year; and the blessing of the God of Jacob!

Yours affectionately,

C. H. SPURGEON

2: LONDON, COURTSHIP AND THE LONG PASTORATE BEGUN

[*James Low, Senior Deacon at New Park Street Chapel*]

Cambridge
January 27, 1854

My dear Sir,

I cannot help feeling intense gratification at the unanimity of the church at New Park Street in relation to their invitation to me. Had I been uncomfortable in my present situation, I should have felt unmixed pleasure at the prospect Providence seems to open up before me; but having a devoted and loving people, I feel I know not how.

When I first ventured to preach at Waterbeach, I only accepted an invitation for three months, on the condition that if, in that time, I should see good reason for leaving, or they on their part should wish for it, I should be at liberty to cease supplying, or they should have the same power to request me to do so before the expiration of the time.

Now, with regard to a six months' invitation from you, I have no objection to the length of time, but rather approve of the prudence of the church in wishing to have one so young as myself on an extended period of probation. But I write, after well weighing the matter, to say positively that I cannot, that I *dare* not, accept an unqualified invitation for so long a time. My objection is not to the length of time of probation, but it ill becomes a youth to promise to preach to a London congregation so long, until he knows *them* and they know *him*. I would engage to supply for three months of that time, and then, should the congregation fail, or the church disagree, I would reserve to myself liberty, without breach of engagement, to retire; and you could, on your part, have the right to dismiss me without seeming to treat me ill. Should I see no reason for so doing, and the church still retain their wish for me, I can remain the other three months, either with or without the formality of a further invitation; but even during that time (the second three months) I should not like to regard myself as a fixture, in case of ill-success, but would only be a supply, liable to a fortnight's dismissal or resignation.

Perhaps this is not business-like, – I do not know; but this is the course I should prefer, if it would be agreeable to the church. Enthusiasm and popularity are often the crackling of thorns, and soon expire. I do not wish to be a hindrance if I cannot be a help.

With regard to coming *at once*, I think I must not. My own deacons just hint that I ought to finish the quarter here; though, by *ought*, they simply, 'Pray do so, if you can.' This would be too long a delay. I wish to help them until they can get supplies, which is only to be done with great difficulty; and as I have given you four Sabbaths I hope you will allow me to give them four in return. I would give them the first and second Sabbaths in February, and two more in a month or six weeks' time. I owe them much for their kindness, although they insist that the debt lies on their side. Some of them hope, and almost pray, that you may be tired in three months, so that I may be again sent back to them.

Thus, my dear Sir, I have honestly poured out my heart to you. You are too kind. You will excuse me if I err, for I wish to do right to you, to my people, and to all, as being not my own, but bought with a price.

I respect the honesty and boldness of the small

minority, and only wonder that the number was not greater.[1] I pray God that, if He does not see fit that I should remain with you, the majority may be quite as much the other way at the end of six months, so that I may never divide you into parties.

Pecuniary matters I am well satisfied with. And now one thing is due to every minister, and I pray you to remind the church of it, namely, that in private, as well as in public, they must all earnestly wrestle in prayer to the God of our Lord Jesus Christ, that I may be sustained in the great work.

I am, with the best wishes, for your health, and the greatest respect,

Yours truly,

C. H. SPURGEON

[*The Rev John Spurgeon*[2]]

Early 1854

. . . me that the people would be back at the first blast of the trumpet which gives a certain sound . . . The people are Calvinistic, and they could not get on with anything else. They raised £100 last week for a city missionary, so that they have the sinews of war. The deacons told me that, if I were there three Sundays, there would be no room anywhere. They say that all the London popular ministers are gospel-men, and are plain, simple and original. They have had most of the good preachers of our denomination out of the country; but they have never asked one of them twice, for they gave them such

---

[1]Five members had voted against the call to the nineteen-year-old youth.
[2]This letter to his father has only survived in incomplete form.

philosophical, or dry, learned sermons, that once was enough. I am the only one who has been asked twice, the only one who has been heard with pleasure by all. I told them they did not know what they were doing, nor whether they were in the body or out of the body; they were so starved, that a morsel of gospel was a treat to them. The portraits of Gill and Rippon – large as life – hang in the vestry. Lots of them said I was Rippon over again.[1]

It is God's doing. I do not deserve it; – they are mistaken. I only mention facts. I have not exaggerated; nor am I very exalted by it, for to leave my own dear people makes it a painful pleasure. God wills it.

The only thing which pleases me is, as you will guess, that I am right about College. I told the deacons that I was not a College man, and they said, 'That is to us a special recommendation, for you would not have much savour or unction if you came from College.'

As to a school, or writing to my deacons in case I do not go, I shall feel happiest if left to manage alone, for I am sure that any letter to my deacons would not do any good.[2] A church is free to manage its own affairs. We are in loving unity now, and they will improve. But churches of the Baptist denomination would think it an infringement of their rules and liberties to be touched in the least by persons of other denominations in any matter which is their own concern. I should at once say, and you would not mind my saying so, '*I had nothing to do with the note; I never asked my father to write it; and the deacons must do as they please about laying it before the church.*'

---

[1]John Gill and John Rippon were successively pastors of this Southwark congregation from 1719 to 1836 – Rippon following Gill in 1773 at the age of twenty.

[2]As the letter to his father of Feb. 24, 1852 (above) reveals, John Spurgeon was apprehensive about his son entering upon the gospel ministry with inadequate preparation.

I feel pleasure in the thought that it will not now be necessary, and I feel that, if it had been, I should have been equally contented. Many other ministers have schools; it is a usual thing. It is not right to say, 'If you mean to be a minister;' for I *am* one, and have been for two years as much a minister as any man in England; and probably very much more so, since in that time I have preached more than 600 times.

More soon.

[*The Misses Blunson*]

Borough [Southwark]
March, 1854

My dear Friends,

I have not forgotten you, although I have been silent so long. I have thought of your trials, and have requested of my Master that He would comfort and sustain you. If you have a portion in Him, your troubles will be blessings, and every grief will be turned into a mercy.

I am very well, and everything goes on even better than I could have hoped. My chapel, though large, is crowded; the aisles are blocked up, and every niche is packed as full as possible. I expect to come and see you in about a month. I hope to be at Waterbeach the fourth Sabbath in April. I get on very well in my present lodgings; – but not better than with you, for that would be impossible. I had nothing to wish for better than I had, for your attention to me was beyond all praise. I cannot but feel very much for you, and only wish that I knew how I could serve you.

I hope you will not give way to doubts and despondency; but do what you can, and leave the rest to God. Blessed is the man who has the God of Jacob for his

Helper; he need not fear either want, or pain, or death. The more you can realise this, the happier you become; and the only means for so doing is to hold frequent communion with God in prayer. Get alone with Jesus, and He will comfort your hearts, and restore your weary souls. I hope you have let your rooms. I think I shall stop at Mrs Warricker's; but I will be sure to come and see you, and leave something to remember me by. Trust in God, and be glad, and –

> Believe me to be,
> Yours truly,
> C. H. SPURGEON

[*To the Baptist Church of Christ worshipping in New Park Street Chapel, Southwark*]

> 75, Dover Road
> Borough
> April 28, 1854

Dearly Beloved in Christ Jesus,

I have received your unanimous invitation, as contained in a resolution passed by you on the 19th instant, desiring me to accept the pastorate among you. No lengthened reply is required; there is but one answer to so loving and cordial an invitation. I ACCEPT IT. I have not been perplexed as to what my reply should be, for many things constrain me thus to answer.

   I sought not to come to you, for I was the minister of an obscure but affectionate people; I never solicited advancement. The first note of invitation from your deacons came quite unlooked-for, and I trembled at the idea of preaching in London. I could not understand how it had come about, and even now I am in the hands of our covenant God, whose wisdom directs all things. He shall choose for me; and so far as I can judge, this is His choice.

I feel it to be a high honour to be the Pastor of a people who can mention glorious names as my predecessors, and I entreat of you to remember me in prayer, that I may realise the solemn responsibility of my trust. Remember my youth and inexperience, and pray that these may not hinder my usefulness. I trust also that the remembrance of these will lead you to forgive mistakes I may make, or unguarded words I may utter.

Blessed be the name of the Most High, if He has called me to this office, He will support me in it, – otherwise, how should a child, a youth, have the presumption thus to attempt the work which filled the heart and hands of Jesus?

Your kindness to me has been very great, and my heart is knit unto you. I fear not *your* steadfastness, I fear my own. The gospel, I believe, enables me to venture great things, and by faith I venture this.

I ask your co-operation in every good work; in visiting the sick, in bringing in enquirers, and in mutual edification.

Oh, that I may be no injury to you, but a lasting benefit! I have no more to say, saving this, that if I have expressed myself in these few words in a manner unbecoming my youth and inexperience, you will not impute it to arrogance, but forgive my mistake.

And now, commending you to our covenant God, the Triune Jehovah,

> I am,
> Yours to serve in the gospel,
> C. H. SPURGEON

[*Mr James S. Watts*]

Borough
August 25, 1854

My very dear friend,

I am astonished to find that fame has become so inveterate a fabricator of untruths, for I assure you that I had no more idea of coming to Cambridge on Wednesday than of being dead last week.

I have been, this week, to Tring, in Hertfordshire, on the border of Bucks. I have climbed the goodly hills, and seen the fair vale of Aylesbury below. In the morning, I startled the hare from her form, and at eve talked with the countless stars. I love the glades, and dells, the hills and vales, and I have had my fill of them. The week before, I was preaching at Ramsgate, and then tarried awhile at Margate, and came home by boat. Kent is indeed made to rejoice in her God, for in the parts I traversed, the harvest was luxuriant, and all seemed thankful.

The Crystal Palace is likewise a favourite haunt of mine; I shall rejoice to take your arm one day, and survey its beauties with you.

Now for the cause at New Park Street. We are getting on too fast. Our harvest is too rich for the barn. We have had one meeting to consider an enlargement, – quite unanimous, – meet again on Wednesday, and then a committee will be chosen immediately to provide larger accommodation. On Thursday evenings, people can scarcely find a vacant seat, – I should think not a dozen in the whole chapel. On Sabbath days the crowd is immense, and seat-holders cannot get into their seats; half-an-hour before time, the aisles are a solid block, and many stand through the whole service, wedged in by their fellows, and prevented from escaping by the crowd outside, who seal up the doors, and fill the yard in front, and stand in throngs as far as the sound can reach. I refer mainly to the evening, although the morning is nearly the same.

Souls are being saved. I have more enquirers than I can attend to. From six to seven o'clock on Monday and Thursday evenings, I spend in my vestry; I give but brief interviews then, and have to send many away without being able to see them. The Lord is wondrous in praises. A friend has, in a letter, expressed his hope that my initials may be prophetic, –

C.	H.	S.
COMFORT	HAPPINESS	SATISFACTION

I can truly say they are, for I have *comfort* in my soul, *happiness* in my work, and *satisfaction* with my glorious Lord. I am deeply in debt for your offer of hospitality; many thanks to you. My kindest regards to all my friends, and yours, especially your sons and daughters. I am sure it gives me delight to be remembered by them, and I hope it will not be long before I run down to see them. Hoping you will be *blessed* in going out, and coming in,

> I am,
> Yours truly,
> C. H. SPURGEON

[*Miss Susannah Thompson*[1]]

75, Dover Road
January 11, 1855

My Dearest,

The letter is all I can desire. Oh! I could weep for joy (as I certainly am doing now) to think that my beloved can so well testify to a work of grace in her soul. I knew you were *really* a child of God, but I did not think you had been led in such a path. I see my Master has been ploughing deep, and it is the deep-sown seed, struggling with the clods, which now makes your bosom heave with distress. If I know anything of spiritual symptoms, I think I know a cure for you. Your position is not the sphere for earnest labour for Christ. You have done all you could in more ways than one; but you are not brought into actual contact either with the saints or with the sinful, sick, or miserable, whom you could serve. Active service brings with it warmth, and this tends to remove doubting, for our works thus become evidences of our calling and election.

I flatter no one, but allow me to say, honestly, that few cases which have come under my notice are so satisfactory as yours. Mark, I write not now as your *admiring friend*, but impartially as your Pastor. If the Lord had intended your destruction, He would not have told you such things as these, nor would He enable you so unreservedly to cast yourself upon His faithful promise. As I hope to stand at the bar of God, clear of the blood of all men, it would ill become me to flatter; and as I love you with the deepest and purest affection, far be it from me to trifle with your immortal interests; but I will say

---

[1]Spurgeon had proposed to Susannah on June 10, 1854 and been accepted. They were married on January 8, 1856. See her account in *Early Years*, pp. 277–301.

again that my gratitude to God ought to be great, as well on my own behalf as yours, that you have been so deeply schooled in the lessons of the heart, and have so frequently looked into the charnel-house of your own corruption. There are other lessons to come, that you may be thoroughly furnished; but, oh! my dear one, how good to learn the first lesson well! I loved you once, but feared you might not be an heir of Heaven; – God in His mercy showed me that you were indeed *elect*. I then thought I might without sin reveal my affection to you, – but up to the time I saw your note, I could not imagine that you had seen such great sights, and were so thoroughly versed in soul-knowledge. God is good, very good, infinitely good. Oh, how I prize this last gift, because I now know, more than ever, that the Giver loves the gift, and so I may love it, too, but only in subservience to His. Dear purchase of a Saviour's blood, you are to me a Saviour's gift, and my heart is full to over-flowing with the thought of such continued goodness. I do not wonder at His goodness, for it is just like Him; but I cannot but lift up the voice of joy at His manifold mercies.

Whatever befall us, trouble and adversity, sickness or death, we need not fear a final separation, either from each other, or our God. I am glad you are not here just at this moment, for I feel so deeply that I could only throw my arms around you and weep. May the choicest favours be thine, may the Angel of the Covenant be thy companion, may thy supplications be answered, and may thy conversation be with Jesus in Heaven! Farewell; unto my God and my father's God I commend you.

Yours, with pure and holy affection, as well as terrestrial love,

C.H. SPURGEON

[*Mr James S. Watts*]

Borough
March 23, 1855

My dear Friend and Brother,

Often have I looked for a note from you, but I have not reproached you, for I, too, have been negligent. Really, I never seem to have an hour to call my own. I am always at it, and the people are teasing me almost to death to get me to let them hear my voice. It is strange that such a power should be in one small body to crowd Exeter Hall to suffocation, and block up the Strand, so that pedestrians have to turn down by-ways, and all other traffic is at a standstill.

The Globe, of last evening, says that, never since the days of Whitefield was there such a religious *furor*, and that the glories of Wesley and Whitefield seem in danger of being thrown into the shade. Well, the Press has *kicked* me quite long enough, now they are beginning to *lick* me; but one is as good as the other as long as it helps to fill our place of worship. I believe I could secure a crowded audience at dead of night in a deep snow.

On Fast-day, all Falcon Square was full, – police active, women shrieking, – and at the sight of me the rush was fearful . . . Strange to say, nine-tenths of my hearers are *men*; but one reason is, that *women* cannot endure the awful pressure, the rending of clothes, etc., etc. I have heard of parties coming to the hall, from ten to twelve miles distance, being there half-an-hour before time, and then never getting so much as near the door.

Dear me, how little satisfies the crowd! What on earth are other preachers up to, when, with ten times the talent, they are snoring along with prosy sermons, and sending the world away? The reason is, they do not know what *the gospel* is; they are afraid of *real gospel Calvinism* and therefore the Lord does not own them.

And now for spiritual matters. I have had knocking about enough to kill a dozen, but the Lord has kept me. Somewhere *in nubibus* there lies a vast mass of nebulæ made of advice given to me by friends, – most of it about humility. Now, my Master is the only One Who can humble me. My pride is so infernal that there is not a man on earth who can hold it in, and all their silly attempts are futile; but then my Master can do it, and He will. Sometimes, I get such a view of my own insignificance that I call myself all the fools in the world for even letting pride pass my door without frowning at him. I am now, as ever, able to join with Paul in saying, 'Having nothing yet possessing all things.'

Souls are being converted, and flying like doves to their windows. The saints are more zealous, and more earnest in prayer.

Many of the man-made parsons are mad, and revile me; but many others are putting the steam on, for this is not the time to sleep in.

The Lord is abroad. The enemy trembles. Mark how the devil roars; – see *Era*, last week, a theatrical paper, where you can read about 'EXETER HALL THEATRE' linked with Drury Lane, Princess's, etc. Read the slander in *Ipswich Express* and the *London Empire*. The two latter have made an apology.

What a fool the devil is! If he had not vilified me, I should not have had so many precious souls as my hearers.

I long to come and throw one of my *bombs* into Cambridge; you are a sleepy set, and want an explosion to wake you. (Here omit a gentleman whose initials are J.S.W.) I am coming on Good Friday; is your house still the Bishop's Hostel? Of course it is. Now, DO write me; I love you as much as ever, and owe you a vast debt. Why not come and see me? I know you pray for me.

With Christian love to you, and kind remembrances to all your family,

> I am,
> Yours ever truly,
> C. H. SPURGEON

[*Susannah Thompson*]

> Aberfeldy
> July 17, 1855

My Precious Love,

Your dearly-prized note came safely to hand, and verily it did excel all I have ever read, even from your own loving pen. Well, I am all right now. Last Sabbath, I preached twice, and to sum up all in a word, the services were 'glorious'. In the morning, Dr Patterson's place was crammed; and in the evening, Dr Wardlaw's chapel was crowded to suffocation by more than 2,500 people, while persons outside declared that quite as many went away.[1] My reception was enthusiastic; never was greater honour given to mortal man. They were just as delighted as are the people at Park Street. To-day, I have had a fine drive with my host and his daughter. To-morrow, I am to preach *here*. It is quite impossible for me to be left in quiet. Already, letters come in, begging me to go here, there, and everywhere. Unless I go to the North Pole, I never can get away from my holy labour.

---

[1] After these services in Glasgow, Spurgeon had gone on to Aberfeldy. This was his first visit to Scotland and his first long journey by train.

Now to return to you again, I have had day-dreams of you while driving along, I thought you were very near me. It is not long, dearest, before I shall again enjoy your sweet society, if the providence of God permit. I knew I loved you very much before, but now I feel how necessary you are to me; and you will not lose much by my absence, if you find me, on my return, more attentive to your feelings, as well as equally affectionate. I can now thoroughly sympathise with your tears, because I feel in no little degree that pang of absence which my constant engagements prevented me from noticing when in London. How then must you, with so much leisure, have felt my absence from you, even though you well knew that it was unavoidable on my part! My darling, accept love of the deepest and purest kind from one who is not prone to exaggerate, but who feels that here there is no room for hyperbole. Think not that I weary myself by writing; for, dearest, it is my delight to please you, and solace an absence which must be even more dreary to you than to me, since travelling and preaching lead me to forget it. My eyes ache for sleep, but they shall keep open till I have invoked the blessings from above – mercies temporal and eternal, – to rest on the head of one whose name is sweet to me, and who equally loves the name of her own, her much-loved,

C. H. S.

[*Susannah Thompson*]

[From London, December 1855,
before he left to spend Christmas
with his parents in Colchester]

Sweet One,

How I love you! I long to see you; and yet it is but
half-an-hour since I left you. Comfort yourself in my
absence by the thought that my heart is with you. My
own gracious God bless you in all things, – in heart, in
feeling, in life, in death, in Heaven! May your virtues be
perfected, your prospects realised, your zeal continued,
your love to Him increased, and your knowledge of Him
rendered deeper, higher, broader – in fact, may more
than even *my heart* can wish, or *my* hope anticipate, be
yours for ever! May we be mutual blessings; – wherein I
shall err, you will pardon; and wherein you may mistake,
I will more than overlook.

Yours till Heaven, *and then,* –

C. H. S.

[*Thomas W. Medhurst*][1]

London
September 22, 1855

My dear Brother,

Since your departure, I have been meditating upon the
pleasure of being the means of sending you to so
excellent a scene of preparation for the ministry, and in

[1]Medhurst first approached Spurgeon as one uncertain of his spiritual
condition (see p.69 below). Earlier in the month when this letter was
written he had been baptised on profession of faith and instantly began
street preaching. Believing he was called to the gospel ministry, Spurgeon
began to give him weekly instruction. From this small beginning the
Pastors' College developed and by 1891 eight hundred and forty-five men
had been trained.

prayer to God I have sought every blessing upon you, for I love you very much. Oh, how I desire to see you a holy and successful minister of Jesus! I need not bid you work at your studies; I am sure you will; but be sure to live near to God, and hold very much intercourse with Jesus.

I have been thinking that, when you are gone out into the vineyard I must find another to be my dearly-beloved Timothy, just as you are.

Now I find it no easy task to get money, and I have been thinking I must get friends to give me a good set of books, which I shall not *give* you, but keep for those who may come after; so that, by degrees, I shall get together a good Theological Library for young students in years to come.

If I were rich, I would give you all; but, as I have to bear all the brunt of the battle, and am alone responsible, I think I must get the books to be always used in future. Those you will purchase to-day are yours to keep; Mr Bagster's books must be mine; and I have just written to a friend to buy me Matthew Henry, which shall soon be at your disposal, and be mine in the same way. You see, I am looking forward.

> Believe me,
> Ever your very loving friend,
> C. H. SPURGEON

[*James S. Watts*]

> Borough
> Feb. 23, 1856

My dear Brother,

A wearied soldier finds one moment of leisure to write a despatch to his brother in arms. Eleven times this week have I gone forth to battle, and at least thirteen services are announced for next week. Additions to the church, last year, 282; received this year, in three months, more than 80; – 30 more proposed for next months, – hundreds, who are equally sincere, are asking for admission; but time will not allow us to take in more. Congregation more than immense, – even *The Times* has noticed it. Everywhere, at all hours, places are crammed to the doors. The devil is wide awake, but so, too, is the Master.

The Lord Mayor, though a Jew, has been to our chapel; he came up to my vestry to thank me. I am to go and see him at the Mansion House. The Chief Commissioner of Police also came, and paid me a visit in the vestry; but, better still, some thieves, thimbleriggers, harlots, etc., have come, and some are now in the church, as also a right honourable hot-potato man, who is prominently known as 'a hot Spurgeonite.'

The sale of sermons is going up, – some have sold 15,000. *Wife*, first-rate; beloved by all my people, we have good reason mutually to rejoice.

I write mere heads, for you can fill up details.

I have been this week to Leighton Buzzard, Foots Cray, and Chatham; everywhere, no room for the crowd. Next week, I am to be thus occupied:–

Sabbath	Morning and evening, New Park Street. Afternoon, to address the Schools.
Monday	Morning, at Howard Hinton's Chapel. Afternoon, New Park Street. Evening, New Park Street.
Tuesday	Afternoon Evening Leighton.

| Wednesday | Morning
Evening | Zion Chapel, Whitechapel. |

| Thursday | Morning, Dalston.
Evening, New Park Street |

| Friday | Morning, Dr Fletcher's Chapel.
Evening, Mr Rogers' Chapel, Brixton. |

With best love,
Yours in haste,
C. H. SPURGEON

3: LETTERS OF
COUNSEL AND CONSOLATION

THE URGENCY OF FINDING REAL RELIGION
[*Master William Cooper*[1]]

Cambridge
——, 1851

My dear William,

You see, by this address, that I am no longer at Mr Swindell's, but am very comfortable here in a smaller school of about fifteen boys. I suppose you are at home, but find farming is not all play, nor perhaps altogether so profitable or pleasant as study; it is well said, 'We do not know the value of our mercies till we lose them.'

Knowing, (in some humble measure, at least), the value of religion let me also bring it before your attention. If you give yourself time to think, you will soon remember that you must die; and if you meditate one more moment, you will recollect that you have a soul, and that soul will never die, but will live for ever; and if you die in your present state, it must live in endless torment. You are an accountable being; God, who made you, demands perfect obedience. But you must own that you have sinned; say not 'I am not a great sinner,' for one sin only would be sufficient to sink your soul for ever in the pit of perdition. The sentence of death stands against you, and mercy alone stays its execution. Seeing now that you are in such danger, how do you think to escape?

[1]One of his former pupils at Newmarket.

Surely you will not be content to die as you are, for you will one day find it no light matter to endure the hot displeasure of an angry God. Do you imagine that, if you live better for the future, God will forgive your past offences? That is a mistake; see if you can find it in the Bible.

Perhaps you intend to think about religion after you have enjoyed sin a little longer; or (but surely you are not so foolish) possibly you think that you are too young to die. But who knows whether that future time will be afforded, and who said that you can turn to Christ just when you please? Your heart is deceitful above all things, and your natural depravity so great that you will not turn to God. Trust not, then, to resolutions made in your own strength, they are but wind; nor to yourself, who are but a broken reed; nor to your own heart, or you are a fool. There is no way of salvation but Christ; you cannot save yourself, having no power even to think one good thought; neither can your parents' love and prayers save you; none but Jesus can; He is the Saviour of the helpless, and I tell you that He died for all such as feel their vileness, and come to Him for cleansing.

You do not deserve salvation; well, there is not a jot of merit on the sinner's part mentioned in the covenant. You have nothing; you are nothing; but Christ is all, and He must be everything to you, or you will never be saved. None reach Heaven, but by free-grace, and through free-grace alone. Even a faint desire after any good thing came from God, from Whom you must get more, for He giveth liberally, and no poor sinner, begging at His door, was ever yet sent empty away.

Look at the blessedness of real religion, no one is truly happy but a child of God. The believer is safe, for God has promised to preserve him; and if once you have the pearl of great price, it cannot be taken from you. The way to Heaven is faith, 'looking unto Jesus'; this faith is the gift of God, and none but those who have it know its value. Oh, may you possess it! – is the earnest prayer of –

Yours faithfully,
CHARLES. H. SPURGEON

ADVICE TO AN ENQUIRER
[*Thomas W. Medhurst*]

Borough
July 14, 1854

Dear Sir,

I am glad that you have been able to write to me and state your feelings. Though my hands are always full, it will ever give me joy to receive such notes as yours.

You ask me a very important question, '*Are you one of God's elect?*' Now, this is a question neither you nor I can answer at present, and therefore let it drop. I will ask you an easier one, '*Are you a sinner?*' Can you say 'YES'? All say, 'Yes'; but then they do not know what the word 'sinner' means.

A sinner is a creature who has broken all his Maker's commands, despised His Name, and run into rebellion against the Most High. A sinner deserves hell, yea, the hottest place in hell; and if he be saved, it must be entirely by unmerited mercy. Now, if you are such a sinner, I am glad to be able to tell you the only way of salvation, 'Believe on the Lord Jesus.'

I think you have not yet really understood what believing means. You are, I trust, really awakened, but you do not see the door yet. I advise you seriously to be much alone, I mean as much as you can; let your groans go up if you cannot pray, attend as many services as possible; and if you go with an earnest desire for a blessing, it will come very soon. But why not believe now? You have only to believe that Jesus is able and willing to save, and then trust yourself to Him.

Harbour not that dark suggestion to forsake the house of God; remember you turn your back on Heaven, and your face to hell, the moment you do that. I pray God that He will keep you. If the Lord had meant to destroy you, He would not have showed you such things as these. If you are but as smoking flax, there is hope. Touch the hem of His garment; look to the brazen serpent.

My dear fellow-sinner, slight not this season of awakening. Up, and be in earnest. It is your soul, your OWN soul, your eternal welfare, your Heaven or your hell, that is at stake.

There is the cross, and a bleeding God-man upon it; look to Him, and be saved! There is the Holy Spirit able to give you every grace. Look, in prayer, to the Sacred Three-one-God, and then you will be delivered.

> I am,
> Your anxious friend,
> C. H. SPURGEON

FURTHER ADVICE ON MAKING SURE OF SALVATION
[*Thomas W. Medhurst*]

> 75, Dover Road
> August 7, 1854

My dear Sir,

Your letters have given me great joy. I trust I see in you the marks of a son of God, and I earnestly pray that you may have the evidence within that you are born of God.

There is no reason why you should not be baptised. 'If thou believest with all thine heart, thou mayest.' Think very seriously of it, for it is a solemn matter. Count the cost. You are now about to be buried to the world, and you may well say, 'What manner of persons ought we to be in all holy conversation and godliness.'

The friends who were with you in the days of your carnal pleasure will strive to entice you from Christ; but I pray that the grace of God may be mightily manifest in you, keeping you steadfast, unmovable, always abounding in the work of the Lord.

I should like to see you on Thursday evening, after six o'clock, in the vestry.

> I am,
> Yours faithfully,
> C. H. SPURGEON

ON BEGINNING MISSIONARY SERVICE
[*Mr N. H. Patrick*]

> Menton
> Dec. 14

Dear Mr Patrick,

I rejoice that the way is cleared for your going to North Africa. As a brother looking to our own funds for support you are the first representative of the Foreign Mission of the College, and I am the more earnest that you should lead the way gloriously.[1] I am sure from your

---

[1]The date of this letter is uncertain. Patrick was not the first Tabernacle missionary but apparently the first sent out by the Pastors' College Missionary Association. He was supported by the Tabernacle for many years along with others in Germany, China, Spain and North Africa.

personal character, and from your course in College that I may place unlimited confidence in you; and far more is my confidence in the Lord whom you and I unitedly serve with our whole hearts. He will help you to play the man. A blend of zeal, patience, and wisdom will be needed in a mission so new, dealing with such a peculiar people. You believe that *the Gospel* will meet the need of any creature in the form of man, whether Jew or Gentile, Mahometan or heathen. You will keep wholly and only to the cross. There hangs our hope, as well as the hope of those to whom we go. Hammer away with the old Gospel; and let those who like it use the miserable wooden mallet of mere reason. The Lord will be with you. Take special care to be much with HIM. Without the means of grace, in a lone land, as you will probably be ere long, 'give attention to reading' the one and only book, and be often carried away to heaven on the wings of prayer and meditation.

Write us often that you may keep up the interest of the brethren, and of my constituency in the glorious work. Be of good courage while you are dumb in the language of the people, and feel the fire burning within with the power to let its heat warm the people. Carry your daily worries to your Master and they will not be worries. Aspire to be another 'Patrick' – the apostle of North Africa, as he was of Ireland.

On your head may the Holy Spirit pour of the anointing oil, and may you often be constrained to sing as I do, –

> *O to grace how great a debtor*
> *Daily I'm constrained to be.*

God himself bless you.

Yours in Christ Jesus,
C. H. SPURGEON

SYMPATHY FOR 'A FATHER IN THE GOSPEL'
[*Pastor James Wells*[1]]

Clapham
March 11, 1871

My Dear Friend,

I must apologise for intruding upon your sick chamber, and must beg you not to be troubled by it; but I am very anxious to know how you are, and shall be very grateful if some friend will inform me. I had hoped that your sickness was but a temporary affliction and would soon pass away, but now I hear conflicting rumours.

I assure you of my deep sympathy in your protracted confinement from the labour which is so dear to your heart. Only to be kept out of the pulpit is a bitter sorrow, even could the bed be one of entire rest. I fear, however, that you are enduring days and nights of languishing; and I pray the Lord, the tender lover of our souls, to lay under you His supporting arms. He comforts omnipotently, and no griefs linger when He bids them fly. He breaks us down, and while we lie prostrate He makes us glad to have it so, because His will is done.

You, who have so long been a father in the Gospel, are no novice in the endurance of trial, and I trust that you will be enabled to play the man as thoroughly in lonely suffering as in public service. Immutable purposes and infinite love have been themes of your constant ministry to others. May the Holy Ghost make these mighty floods

[1]James Wells, now aged sixty-nine, had been in the ministry for forty years and was the best-known Baptist preacher in South London at the time of Spurgeon's settlement in 1854. As a hyper-Calvinist, Wells believed that faith was not a duty which should be preached to sinners. He criticised Spurgeon's teaching on that account and declined any public association. The two men had never met. Shortly after this letter Spurgeon was present at his burial 'though not', says T. W. Medhurst, 'as an invited mourner'. See *Life and Work of C. H. Spurgeon*, G. H. Pike, vol. 5, pp. 34–35.

of consolation to roll in upon your own soul, till all things else are swallowed up in your heart's holy joy! Personally I own my great obligations to the furnace and the hammer; and I am sure that you also rejoice in the assurance that tribulation worketh patience, and brings, through the supply of the Spirit, a long train of blessings with it. May you be delivered from all excessive care as to your church and your work – the Lord's work is safe in the Lord's hands. Happy is it for us when we can feel it to be so. May your sick chamber be the very gate of heaven to your soul, the presence of the Lord filling the house with glory.

Do not think of acknowledging this; but if you are able to have it read to you I hope someone will be so good as briefly to tell me how you are.

With most sincere respects,
yours truly,
C. H. SPURGEON

THE SHOCK OF THE UNEXPECTED

Clapham
July 25, 1874

Dear Friend,

I am deeply grieved by the sad news which has just arrived by telegram. It is unexpected indeed. I pray that your will may run side by side with that of your Lord, and may you even thank Him, 'for so it seemed good in Thy sight.' We can see no reason or goodness in the removal because we are quite unable to see afar off, but faith knows that there is both wisdom and love in it, and leaves all to the far-seeing Lord. The Comforter will be with you; a deeper experience of trial will prepare you for greater heights of service. Sharp pruning will increase sweet fruit.

> With the utmost love,
> Your sympathising friend,
> C. H. SPURGEON

ON LIVING BY FAITH

> Westwood
> March 9, '81

Dear Friend,

You seem to me to be in the night school, – by no means pleasant lessons, few holidays, and no cakes and sugar-sticks; – but a wise Teacher, and a guarantee of becoming a well-trained disciple in due time. This is much better than to be pampered with joyous excitements, and to be thereby really weakened in faith. How could you honour Christ, by trusting Him as He is revealed in Scripture, if you were always having new revelations over and above His Word? Too much sight renders faith impossible. A certain measure of darkness is needful for the full exercise of faith. Be of good comfort; for He who has redeemed you will not lose that which has cost Him so much. I hope you will yet recover strength. Why, you are only a young girl yet at thirty-seven! But I know how the spirits sink, and one feels as old as Methuselah. The Lord be ever your Comforter!

> Yours, with much to do,
> C. H. SPURGEON

HOME IN SIGHT
[*The Rev Thomas Curme*]

Westwood
June 12, 1884

Dear Friend,

I casually heard from Mr Abraham that you were ill, but I had no idea that it was a serious matter; but Mr Rochfort has kindly given me further news. I feel very sad about it, but I am sure you do not. The loss will be ours, and Heaven and you will gain.

Dear loving brother, you have nothing now to do but to go home; and what a home! You will be quite at home where all is love, for you have lived in that blessed element, and are filled with it. I shall soon come hobbling after you, and shall find you out. We are bound to gravitate to each other whether here or in glory. We love the same Lord, and the same blessed truth.

May the everlasting arms be underneath you! I breathe for you a loving, tender prayer, – 'Lord, comfort Thy dear servant, and when he departs, may it be across a dried-up river into the land of living fountains!'

I am fifty next Thursday, and you are near your Jubilee. In this we are alike; but Jesus is the highest joy. Into the Father's hands I commit you, 'until the day break, and the shadows flee away.'

Your loving brother,
C. H. SPURGEON

THE RULE FOR PEACE–MAKERS

Nightingale Lane
Clapham
Feb. 5

Bear. Bear. Bear.
Forbear. Forbear. Forbear.

In yielding is victory. Fight the devil and love the deacon – Love him till he is loveable.

Yours heartily,
C. H. SPURGEON

ON LOSING A CHILD
[*Mr W. Higgs Jr.*[1]]

Westwood
Mar. 18, 1886

Dear Friend,

I feel very grieved for you and the dear wife, for I know your tender hearts. Yet the bitterest elements of sorrow are not in the cup, for we have no doubt as to where little ones must be.

You have now a child among the angels – to whom we will soon go. So short is life that our wounds are staunched almost as soon as they begin to bleed. We part, and so soon meet.

Mrs Spurgeon joins with me in loving sympathy.

Yours in our Lord Jesus,
C. H. SPURGEON

[1] Son of William Higgs, builder of the Metropolitan Tabernacle and one of its most trusted deacons.

FRIENDSHIP IN LIFE AND DEATH

> Westwood
> Beulah Hill
> Upper Norwood
> Aug. 18, 1886

Dear Brother Court,[1]

Mr William Olney passed through the operations very wonderfully. His spirits never flagged, and his faith was ever firm and joyous. He has gone to Tunbridge Wells to rest, and I expect him back vigorous as ever.[2] Bless the Lord!

It is a great pleasure to hear from you, my dear brother. Infirmities multiply, but grace abides unalterable. You are in the best of keeping. The tent is being taken down; it has been a first-rate one to last for 86 years. The house of God not made with hands will be a far better dwelling for you.

The Lord bless you evermore. Should you ever need temporal help, you know that I am not behind-hand.

> Yours heartily,
> C. H. SPURGEON

[1] Court, who was an elder at the Tabernacle, died the following year. This letter is characteristic of Spurgeon's close relationship with all his office bearers.

[2] William Olney, as his father before him, was senior deacon at the Tabernacle and a close friend. He died in 1890 after being a member of the church for fifty-four years.

FIRST STEPS FOR A WOULD-BE MISSIONARY

Westwood
Beulah Hill
Upper Norwood
Sep. 9, 1887

Dear Sir,

Are you a member of a Baptist church? Then see your Pastor. He will tell you that before you apply for foreign work you must prove your qualifications at home. This involves your beginning to preach in Street or somewhere. It will be best to consult your Pastor, for details may need to be talked over.

Yours truly,
C. H. SPURGEON

4: TO FELLOW PASTORS
AND
FELLOW WORKERS

Clapham
Saturday evening
July 26, 1862

My dear Mr Medhurst,

You know how cautious I must be about advising any removes, for I am sure to be charged with taking you away from Coleraine; therefore act this time on your own responsibility. I would lay it before the Lord, judge deliberately, and act decisively. I have a very strong impression that you will go to Glasgow. I will not venture to say more.

You will, I know, quite feel that my love for you is as deep and sincere as ever. I shall ever value *my first-born* above all the rest. Now I am going to give you a proof of my true love in a very plain remark. I notice that you have fallen into a very bad mannerism in speaking. Where did you catch it? You used to speak roughly, but it was always pleasant to listen to your voice; but several friends have mentioned, what I also noticed, a sort of ministerial tone, a genteel way of pulling the tails of some of the words and cutting the ears of others, till they look like little dogs fresh from the fancier's. Now YOU must not have a single flaw. You are so good and so manly that I cannot let you fall into these mannerisms. You will do good and be eminent, but this wheel in your carriage, when I tap it with my critical hammer, does not ring right. Just come back to Old John Bull's way of utterance, and be a Paddy no longer.

There, don't think this too severe; I only meant to knock a fly off.

If you go to Glasgow, the people there ought to treat you handsomely in point of salary. I would suggest, as a sort of set-off to your loss from Coleraine, that the Glasgow church make a handsome donation towards the Coleraine Chapel, if that projected building be erected. I think W—— would cheerfully go to Coleraine, and might not be an unsuitable person.

Next, in reference to ——'s church, I must beg you, overlooking all shortcomings, to regard him as a brother labourer and his church as one of our fraternity. I hope ever to see all our churches perfectly one in heart. The time approaches for the formation of a distinct body or confederation, and to have two large interests in Glasgow will be noble indeed, if they agree in one.

We had such a meeting last night. The Lord is with the College. We only want faith, and that is growing. We will fill the nation with the Gospel, and then send our armies out the wide world over.

Big words, but written in faith in a great God.

God bless you and yours.

Yours ever lovingly,
C. H. SPURGEON

[*T. W. Medhurst*]

Clapham, S.W.
August 2, 1869

My dear Friend,

I suppose you maun be flittin', but it's nae weel for Glasgie. God be wi' ye.

C. H. SPURGEON

[*To the Assembly of the United Methodist Free Churches*]

August, 1871

Brethren in Christ,

Your letter, dated July 28, has only reached me on the evening of this day (31), hence my apparent neglect in answering is not a real one. I thank you heartily for the kind invitation, and should have endeavoured to avail myself of it but for two personally painful reasons. First, I am not yet equal to an 'Assembly dinner'. The glow of fraternal excitement would utterly overcome me. What little strength I have – and it is yet but little – I spend in preaching, and you will all agree it is the best form in which to lay it out. Second, at the hour of your love-feast I shall be on the way to a grave which is to hold the dear remains of a deacon, worthy and beloved, who has lately fallen asleep in Jesus. So I cannot be with you in person; but I have paused at this moment to breathe a prayer that the Lord's love, light, and life may abound in your holy gatherings, and that you may return to your spheres of labour clothed with the Holy Spirit's power. I know not in what better way I can serve you. May we, dear brethren, be all the more quickened to the fullest degree of spiritual life. We require all the spiritual energy that can be had, in order that our work for the Lord may tell upon our times. We must press hard on the graving-tool or it will leave no mark on this age of brass, and we cannot throw out more force than is first placed within us from above. Few of us rise to the sacred ardour of flaming love which Jesus' wounds claim of us. Conscious that I fall far short, I look anxiously to see the uprise of heaven-born zealots who shall be eaten up with the zeal of the Lord's house. Whether the Lord sends these to the United Methodist Free Churches or to the Baptists, we shall all be the better for them. Therefore we will join in praying for the coming of such, and aim to be such ourselves. Excuse this little written speech, and believe me to be, to you and all who love our Lord, a true brother and hearty well-wisher.

C. H. SPURGEON

[*The Rev James Archer Spurgeon*[1]]

Off Arran
Saturday, July 27, 1878

Dear Brother,

I have suffered so greatly . . . that I can hardly tell whether I am benefited or not by this change. Yet it ought to be a great boon to me, for fresh air, fine scenery,

---

[1]James Spurgeon, unlike his brother, trained for the Baptist ministry at Stepney College and thereafter was a pastor in Southampton and Bayswater Rd., London. From 1867 to Charles's death, James Spurgeon served as co-pastor of the Metropolitan Tabernacle, with responsibility for pastoral work and administration rather than for the preaching. The latter was generally undertaken by his elder brother. C. H. Spurgeon had been ill in the summer of 1878.

and cheerful company make up a powerful medicine. M. will have told you how we have got on.

Preaching four sermons is not a help to rest; yet the people are so eager to hear that it ought to be a delight to me.

I trust there will be a large number to receive into fellowship when I return. It is wonderful how the increase has been sustained for so long. I can scarcely hope to see it remain at the highest level, and yet I should mourn its decrease.

I hope your dear wife remains better, and that your trial in that direction may be succeeded by great joy. May you long continue strong and well. With my poor creaking machine, which only holds together with difficulty, it was kind on our Lord's part to find me a brother so vigorous in all ways.

Yours, with hearty love,
CHARLES

[*The Rev James Archer Spurgeon*]

My dear Brother,

Will you kindly tell the friends how sorry I am that I cannot come to the prayer meeting. Instead of doing my sermon I have had to be in the Old Bailey Court all day for no good whatever. I have the sermon to do tonight and then three engagements tomorrow. I feel tired and weary and full of head-ache and must go home. May the Spirit of God be with you and may the meeting bring down infinite blessing upon the work.

Yours truly,
C. H. SPURGEON

[*J. L. Keys*][1]

Nightingale Lane
Balham, Surrey
Sept. 13, '79

Dear Mr Keys,

I am half ashamed to write about common things while your sorrow is on you, but possibly it may not be unwise after all.

I want a good and cheap copy of Gill's Commentary for my son Charles. Whitefield's sermons – the one by Legg, and also Lange on Gospels if you can get them pretty cheap in the 7 vols edition. These are for a birthday present for next Friday and must not be very shabby but of course are secondhand.

In the midst of your sorrows and expenses be not too much burdened. If you find yourself too much pressed there is another £10 to be had.

From

Yours in much sympathy,
C. H. SPURGEON

[1]Keys acted as an editorial secretary, researcher and proof-reader for Spurgeon. All the preacher's many publications from 1867 to 1891 passed through his hands – 'his suitability and efficiency are beyond all praise' (*C. H. Spurgeon, Autobiography, vol. 2: The Full Harvest, 1860–1892*, Banner of Truth Trust, 1973, p. 190). Keys died in 1899.

[Pastor William Williams][1]

Westwood
Beulah Hill
Upper Norwood
Jan. 21, 1881

Dear Friend,

Harrold[2] will be away tomorrow and I shall be all alone –
not over bright. Can you leave the queen at the Crown,
the circle at the Oval, and come and see one who is ill on
the hill, and would be glad to see you.

Yours truly,

C. H. SPURGEON

[W. Y. Fullerton and J. M. Smith][3]

Westwood
Sept. 13, 1883

Dear Brethren,

I rejoice that you have begun so hopefully in Bury, may
you see the Lord's hand more and more plainly every
day. Oh, for thousands of real conversions! We want no
sham penitents, and noisy professors; but men and
women whose hearts are sick of sin, and whose minds

[1]A friend and colleague of Spurgeon's in South London. On Spurgeon's
day off (Wednesday) they sometimes went out into the country together.
See *Personal Reminiscences of C. H. Spurgeon*, William Williams, Religious
Tract Society, London, 1895.

[2]Joseph W. Harrald, trained in the Pastors' College, had become a pastor
in Shoreham before becoming Spurgeon's personal secretary in the late
1870s. See *The Rev. Joseph William Harrald*, A. Harwood Field, Arthur H.
Stockwell, London, n.d.

[3]Fullerton and Smith were evangelists connected with the Metropolitan
Tabernacle Evangelists' Association.

find real rest in Jesus. This must be the work of the Holy Ghost, and therefore the godly must pray mightily for you. All must begin and end at the throne of grace. You and I know this, and have felt the truth of it; and therefore we put it in the forefront of the battle.

Give my love to the Lord's servants who are helping you, and bid them ask great things from the great God. Why should we look for so little and reap so little? The God of Pentecost is with us.

Yours in much love,
C. H. SPURGEON

Westwood
Beulah Hill
Upper Norwood
S.E.
June 17, 1884

Dear Mr Page,

I thank you and your people with all my heart. I intend to give YOU as a birthday Jubilee present a complete set of Calvin. I believe the books will be at Tabernacle by Thursday and if so you will want a cab to take them home. You have earned them so there will be no need of thanks.

Yours ever lovingly,
C. H. S.

[*The Rev Alexander Whyte, Edinburgh*]

Westwood
Beulah Hill
Upper Norwood
Sept. 13, 1884

Dear Sir,

By some accident your excellent book on the *Shorter Catechism* has escaped me. I earnestly apologise for the oversight, especially as I greatly value the inscription that you have placed in the copy.

I have been a prisoner through illness again, and so I have been using up review-books. Hence yours was routed out. Thank you for it. It is a right good, live book. It has done me good to read it, I am glad that some one loves sound doctrine as I do. I am beginning to be banned as a stupid old fogey, who sticks in the mud, and will not advance. When they have gone round the whirligig they will pass some of us again, but they will there and then again begin to be behind us, and not before us as they dream.

May your handbook do real service among your own countrymen. Alas, these degenerate lowlands know not 'the *Shorter Catechism*', and this makes them all the shorter of grace and truth.

Yours heartily,
C. H. SPURGEON

Westwood
Beulah Hill
Upper Norwood
Jan. 23, 1885

Dear Friend,

Can you come to London, and preach for me, or for my people if I am dead, on Feb 22? I have been waiting three weeks to move off, but I am still a prisoner – better, however. It would make me feel easier if I had the Sundays all arranged for again. My plans have been broken, and my purposes crossed, and yet it is well. God be praised.

Do help me if you can. My claim is – that I am in need, that I have no claim on you whatever, and that I can never repay you. Fine scope for grace here!

> Yours ever heartily,
> C. H. SPURGEON

> London
> May 18, [?]

My dear Bro,

I have long desired to collect about 50 hymns on the second coming which with 50 more of my own favourites not in Rippon upon other subjects I want to make into a small selection for my own prayer meetings.

Now if you will let me have those you collect, I am too busy to get them together but any small remuneration you might desire should be cheerfully given and you could yet use them in your proposed volume which if it meets my views I pledge myself to recommend and will do anything towards its sale – which lies in my power – what say you? I should want the 50 hymns to be in 'Spurgeon's Selection for the meetings of the saints.' Will you arrange 50 for me and if you like I will acknowledge you as the compiler of that portion of my little volume.

I do not want them very millenarian, I want SECOND ADVENT Hymns – not in Watts nor in Rippon.

With great Xn regard believe me,

> Yours in the coming Messiah,
> C. H. SPURGEON

[*The Rev James Archer Spurgeon*]

Westwood
June 7, 1887

Dear Brother,

I desire for you all that you can desire for yourself and more. It has been a great joy to have you for a brother, not in flesh nor in name merely, but in the fulness of the truth, – in very deed and heart. However much *I* may have failed in my part, *you* have done yours to the full, in a way which I can better appreciate than describe. I am not able to remember a jarring feeling between us, and I do not suppose there ever will be one. Certainly the chances of it, if they ever existed, are effectually extinguished by the rare felicity of your choice in your present wedded state. *Your* wife was *my* friend long before you made her my sister, and certainly no brother or sister could be more desirable than you twain.

Length of days, domestic bliss, bodily health, mental vigour, and heart repose are among the smallest of the blessings which I ask for you.

I have joined others in two ways in the tokens of regard which will be mere hints of the respect in which you are held. Our love is with you ever.

Your loving brother,
C. H. SPURGEON

[*Pastor George Samuel*]

> Westwood
> Beulah Hill
> Upper Norwood
> Sept. 25, 1888

Dear Mr Samuel,

I voted for New Zealand in my last – now let me write the other side.

A voyage might be too trying for you. The Canal is awful for ill people. The voyage would be little or no real *rest*.

There are thousands of rooms to be had at Menton. What I wanted to know for was to write and make a bargain for you at my Hotel, for I should greatly like your company. I have no fear of your intrusion. Bless you. You would be within 30 hours of home if you were ill, or your family needed you home. You would not be all alone, nor tempted to run down in spirit.

I half hope that I shall have you with me; but yet consider only yourself, – for there is no need to consider *me*, and in considering yourself only you do me the greatest service.

8 fr. per diem would I think include board, lodging, and service.

My room would be at your service in the day when you were indoors.[1]

With hearty love,

> Yours truly,
> C. H. SPURGEON

[1]A further letter of Spurgeon's of November 2, 1888, reveals that Pastor Samuel of Birmingham decided to go to the Antipodes.

[*Pastor William Williams*]

Westwood
1888

Dear Mr Williams,

Could you give lecture tomorrow at college at 2.30? My mother is dead, and I feel very low. If you can, please wire me first thing.

You could be done by four for your meeting.

Yours very heartily,
C. H. SPURGEON

Westwood
Beulah Hill
Upper Norwood
Feb. 28, 1889

Dear Mr Smith,

I do not think there can be any doubt about your going to Farringdon. *Go,* and *the Lord be with you.* I rejoice much to see this church standing fast, and that you should go and confirm them in the faith. I suppose you will continue with us till quarter day: but go when you please.

You have my cheerful consent, and heartiest prayers.

Yours in Christ Jesus,
C. H. SPURGEON

[*N. H. Patrick*]

Westwood
Beulah Hill
Upper Norwood
May 17, 1890

Dear Mr Patrick,[1]

Rio should restore the money, or part of it, as he is able. He ought not to get off scot free. I do not see how the Bank is clear, for they ought not to have paid it to any one unless he has a banking account. I think something must be done with the Bank.

I send enclosed the usual cheque. Would you like *Lainez* to join you? He is in the College, and is applying to the Bapt Mission, but as he speaks Spanish, and comes from San Domingo, he is the man to help you.

The Lord be ever with you, and give you true converts in lieu of the pretender! My heart's love is with you.

Yours heartily,
C. H. SPURGEON

£12.10.0 for salary to end of May.
£12.10.0 for 4th quarter's rent of Café.

[*The Rev J. A. Spurgeon*]

Westwood
October 18, 1890

Dear Brother,

We have a stiff week before us. Monday, at 3.0, laying stone. Tuesday, at Malden, at 11.0. Wednesday, funeral

---

[1]Missionary in North Africa, see above, p.71.

at Tabernacle, at 2.0. Will you go to the house, 12.30, and to the grave? I will preach in Tabernacle.

I cannot see how I am to get an address for teachers on Monday night, and get my sermon done in the morning before I start for Penrose Street. The Lord help us.

With much love,

C. H. S.

5: TO HIS OWN
CHILDREN
AND OTHERS

Cambridge
Thursday, Dec., 1850

Miss Caroline Louisa Spurgeon,[1]

Your name is so long that it will almost reach across the paper. We have one young gentleman in our school whose name is Edward Ralph William Baxter Tweed; the boys tease him about his long name; but he is a very good boy, and that makes his name a good one. Everybody's name is pretty, if they are good people. The Duke of Tuscany has just had a little son; the little fellow was taken to the Catholic Cathedral, had some water put on his face, and then they named him – you must get Eliza to read it, – Giovanni Nepomerceno, Maria Annunziata Giuseppe Giovanbattista Ferdinando Baldassere Luigi Gonzaga Pietro Alessandro Zanobi Antonino. A pretty name to go to bed and get up with; it will be a long time before he will be able to say it all the way through! If anyone is called by the name of Christian, that is better than all these great words: it is the best name in the world, except the name of our Lord Jesus Christ. My best love to you. I hope you will enjoy yourself, and try to make others happy, too; for then you are sure to be happy yourself; whereas, if you only look out to please yourself, you will make others uncomfortable, and will not make even yourself happy. However,

---

[1]Louisa, Spurgeon's sister, was five years of age at this date.

of course, you know that, and I need not tell you of it. A happy Christmas to you!

> Your loving brother,
> CHARLES

[*Charles Spurgeon*[1]]

Heligoland
Sept., 1867

My dear Charlie,

I am very glad that you wrote a nice little note to your dear mother, and I hope it is a sign that you are always going to be diligent and thoughtful, and this will be a glad thing indeed. . . . I am delighted to hear that you are doing so well at College.[2] Give my love to all the students, and tell Mr Rogers that it always cheers me to know that the brethren bear me up in their prayers.

On this little island there is a lighthouse; you see it at the top, on the left of the picture. It is much needed, for many vessels are wrecked here. We live down below, on the beach, near the square tower with a flag on it; that is a bath-house. Steamers come every two days, and then we can send letters; at other times, we are far off from everybody, alone in the wide, wide sea. We have sheep's milk, for there is no room for cows. Fish is very plentiful, and very good.

My dear boy, I trust that you will prove, by the whole of your future life, that you are truly converted to God. Your actions must be the chief proof. Remember, trees

[1]Spurgeon's twin sons, Charles and Thomas, were born September 20, 1856.

[2]The two boys were being tutored by one of the students who belonged to the Pastors' College, Harry R. Brown, later a missionary in India.

are known by their fruit, and Christians by their deeds. God bless you for ever and ever! Mother sends her kindest love, and so does

Your loving father,

C. H. SPURGEON

[*Charles Spurgeon*]

Rome
Nov. 3, 1868[?]

My very dear Boy,

I have had a very happy journey and am very much better. You can trace my journey thus: I have been in stately Brussels, sniffed in odoriferous Cologne, slept in Rhine-washed Mayence, inspected regal Munich, rested in rustic Botzen, floated in palatial Venice, eaten sausage in Bologna, roamed in flowery Florence, and tarried in imperial Rome. Everywhere protected and blessed of God, I am most grateful, and desire to come back strong for the service of God.

One of my sweetest joys is to hear that a spirit of prayer is in your school, and that you participate in it. To know that you love the Lord and are mighty in prayer would be my crowning joy, and the hope that you do so already is a happy one to me. Dear boy, I should like you to *preach*, but it is best that you *pray*. Many a preacher has proved a castaway, but never one person who had truly learned to pray.

Be careful that your life is consistent with your prayers. You and your brother are differently constituted, and have different temptations, but God is able to bless you both alike, and I pray that He may do so richly.

I wish you were with me here, for you are a nice companion, and if your dear mother were here, too, it would be a joyous day. We will pray to God for her daily.

Give my regards to Mr Olding. Receive my love for yourself.

> Your loving father,
> C. H. SPURGEON

[*Young People at the Metropolitan Tabernacle*]

> Menton
> Jan. 23, 1874

My dear Young Friends,

I am delighted to hear that you came together in such large numbers last Monday in my absence, for I hope it shows a real and deep anxiety among the seekers to find the Saviour, and among the saved ones to plead for others. You do not need the voice of any one man to secure your attention; the Word of the Lord Jesus, by whomsoever spoken, is life and power. It is to Him that you must turn all your thoughts. Sin has separated between you and your God, and Christ alone can bring you back to your Heavenly Father. Be sure that you remember what it cost Him to prepare the way of reconciliation; nothing but His blood could have done it, and He gave it freely, bowing His head to death upon the tree. It must have been no light matter which cost the Redeemer such a sacrifice; I beseech you, do not make light of it. Hate the sin which caused Him so much agony, and yield to the love which sustained Him under it.

I hear that in London you have had fogs and rain, here it is all flowers and summer, and the difference reminds me of the change which faith makes in the soul. While we are unbelievers, we dread the wrath of God, and walk in gloom; but when we believe, we have peace with God, and enjoy His favour, and the spring of an eternal summer has commenced. May the Spirit of God, like the soft south wind, breathe upon you, and make your hearts bloom with desires, blossom with hopes, and bring forth fruits of repentance! From Jesus He proceeds, and to Jesus He leads the soul. Look to Him. Oh, look to Him; to Him alone; to Him simply; to Him at once!

>Your anxious friend,
>C. H. SPURGEON

[*Thomas Spurgeon*]

>Menton
>1877

My dear son Tom,

I am very sorry that you are feeling so weak, and as your dear Mother thinks a voyage would do you good I cannot but yield to the wish. I am rather afraid that it will be too severe a remedy, but I shall not demur to its being tried. If it ends in your going in for the college course and coming into the ministry I shall not regret it; indeed, I shall rejoice if you went round the world seven times if it ended so.

You will preach, I am sure, but without good training you cannot take the position which I want you to occupy. Theology is not to be learned in its amplitude and accuracy by one destined to be a public instructor without going thoroughly into it, and mastering its terms and details. Perhaps a voyage may give tone to your system and prepare you for two years of steady application. Only may the Lord make you a great soul-winner, and I shall be more than content.[1]

We meet some awful donkeys when travelling, but a lady at San Remo is beyond all others. She said that she regretted that our Lord Jesus was a Jew. When asked if she would have preferred his being an Englishman she replied, 'No, but you see it is such a pity that he was a Jew: it would have been far better if he had been a Christian like ourselves'!!

Your loving father,

C. H. SPURGEON

[*Charles Spurgeon*]

Menton
Jan. 15, 1881

My dear Son,

May you some quarter of a century hence enjoy the great pleasure of having your son Charles to preach for you. Mind you must keep up the name – bad as it is.

It is a great delight to me to receive such loving letters from the Bishop of Greenwich[2] who is also my son and

---

[1]Thomas, who with his brother Charles had been baptised at the Tabernacle in 1874, went to Australia later this year. Owing to the illness of his mother he came home in 1878 when he studied for a time at the Pastors' College before returning to the Antipodes in October 1879. In the 1890's he became his father's successor. Spurgeon – as his own father before him – was clearly apprehensive that his gifted son would have insufficient preparation for the ministry, a concern which seems justified by Thomas' subsequent ministry.

[2]After training at the Pastors' College, Charles was now a pastor in Greenwich.

heir, and it is even more joy to see that God is prospering you and making your work successful. I think you have made specially good progress in the time.

Stick to your studies. Read Matthew Henry right through if you can before you are married, for after that event I fear that Jacob may supplant him. Remember me to Mr Huntley and all the good people.

I have not had this week's letter from Tabernacle, and so have not had the eulogiums on your sermons. I am better and better. It is 42 days since we have had rain, and all along the fine weather has been unbroken.

I am so grieved about your dear mother, and my impulse is to come home at once, but then I reflect that I can do her no good, and should do her harm by becoming the second invalid to be waited on. Dear Char, don't get the rheums or the gouts, but spin away on your skates and your cycles. Don't go too much over the bridge, – but you may give my love to Sis.

The sermon was capital. Thank you much.

Your own
DAD

[*Charles Spurgeon*]

Menton
Dec. 12 [?]

My dear Son,

Your note was a real joy to me. What a good fellow you are. I live twice in seeing you so firm in the faith of God's elect. I do not wonder that the chickens flock around the man who gives them real corn and not mere chaff. The Lord keep you evermore true to the truth, and you will see His hand with you more and more.

Your little notices of books are first-rate. Short and pithy – better than half-a-page of long-winded nothings. You may do as many as ever you like, for nobody can do them better, nor as well.

You charm me as I think of your interesting your dear mother, with your views and lantern. It is most sad to have her at home, when I am here, enjoying myself. What can we do but try to cheer her up at home and pray the Lord to give her journeying strength. I am right glad to hear of the growth and advancement of the little girl. God bless her mother.

Yes, I am having a true holiday – not idle, but restful. Our weather here is not so very warm, but just such as to allow of sitting about outdoors. Not many people out here yet. Flowers scarce, since autumn rains did not fall; I hope they are not coming in winter instead.

Love ever to you and yours from,

> Your happy father,
> C. H. S.

[*Stockwell Orphanage Children*[1]]

Menton
December 20, 1887

Dear Boys,

I wish you all a merry Christmas. My son, Mr Charles Spurgeon, will tell you that it is a great trouble to me to be away from you all at Christmas, but I hope you will all enjoy yourselves none the less, and be as happy as kittens. I am very pleased to hear that as a rule you are a good lot of fellows, obedient, teachable, and true; therefore you have a right to be happy, and I hope you are. I always wish everything to be done to make you love the Orphanage and feel it to be your home, and in this all the Trustees join, and so does Mr Charlesworth. We want you to be very jolly while you are with us, and then to grow up and go out into business, and to turn out first-rate men and true Christians.

Boys, give three cheers for the Trustees, who are your best friends, and then the same for Mr Charlesworth, the matrons, and the masters. Don't forget the gentlemen who send the shillings and the figs. Hip, hip, hurrah!

Where are the girls?

Dear Children,

I hope you will be happy too, with Miss Moore and the other kind folks. You cannot make quite so much noise as those uproarious boys, but your voices are very sweet,

---

[1]This Orphanage in Clapham Road, London, originated through Spurgeon's ministry and the gift of a lady belonging to the Church of England in 1866. As its President, Spurgeon retained a constant interest in the children and their spiritual and financial needs were one of the main concerns of his life. Before the end of the last century 527 orphans found a happy home there. Their lives were not regimented or institutionalised. 'The boys and girls are taught to retain their individuality: they are not clothed alike nor shaped in the same mould'. See *C. H. Spurgeon Autobiography, vol. 2: The Full Harvest*, 1973, pp. 161–172.

and I shall be glad one day to hear them when I get well and come home. Enjoy yourselves all you can, and try to make everybody happy in your new home. I hope my first little girls will be specially good ones. Ought not the first to be the best?

Your friend always,
C. H. SPURGEON

[*One of the Orphan Boys*]

Menton
February 5[?]

Dear Bray,—

I was so pleased with your little note. It was so good of you, with all your pain, to sit up and write to me. I hope when the spring weather comes you will feel better, but if not, you know of the 'sweet fields beyond the swelling flood' which 'stand dressed in living green.' The Lord Jesus will be very near you. He feels for dear suffering children. He will keep you patient and joyful. Oh, how He loves! If there is anything you want, be sure to let me know.

Your loving friend,
C. H. SPURGEON

[*Mr and Mrs Charles Spurgeon*]

Westwood
Sept. 11, 1890

My dear Children,

The Lord Himself comfort you. I want comforting myself. To think of that dear little creature being taken away! It must be right! It must be good! Our Father is never mistaken nor unkind.

You are acting wisely in not bringing the little one from the place. You will be setting an example of common sense which is greatly needed in an age which is so sentimental as it is false-hearted.

If you would like a wreath from me, kindly order it in Herne Bay, and send the bill to me. I would try to send one, but if you are not going to have any, I should be setting an ill example.

I feel sure you will both find a secret strength poured into your souls, and in this also faith shall have the victory.

I shall never forget the day. For a wonder your dear mother went with me to the Orphanage, and was very happy. We came home, and the telegram came at once, – just the bitter herbs with the feast.

To you it must be a sharp cut; but our Lord has an almighty salve.

Your loving father,
C. H. SPURGEON

6: THE
PASTORS' COLLEGE

[A Parent]

My dear Sir,

I scarcely wonder at your preference of Regent's Park College for your son,[1] but I think you labour under some mistake, for it so happens that the ground of your choice is just one of the evils which my Institute seeks to remedy.

The residence of a number of young men in one house encourages and necessarily generates levity; their separation from common social life is a serious injury, and tends to unfit them for the wear and tear of future work among ordinary mortals. When a young man resides in a Christian family, not only is he under the most vigilant oversight, but he never ceases to be one of the people. We are far from putting our men into the way of temptation;

---

[1]The development of Spurgeon's College, and its priorities, were certainly somewhat unusual, hence the enquiry to which he is here responding from a parent inclined to favour another better-known Baptist institution. When Spurgeon's first student, T. W. Medhurst (see p.60 above), was joined by a second in 1856, it was arranged that both men live with the Rev George Rogers, a Congregational minister. This was virtually the beginning of the College and thereafter, writes Spurgeon, it 'grew every month and the number of students rapidly advanced from one to forty'. A College building but deliberately without residential accommodation was opened in 1874 and Rogers remained Principal until 1881. Spurgeon was commonly with the men once a week and his *Lectures to My Students* were among the most widely read of all his works.

on the other hand, we think our arrangement is the most effectual method of preservation. I merely write this because your brief acquaintance with our systems may allow me to suppose that this view of the case has not suggested itself to you.

Our tutors are sound scholars; but, as we do not aim at any very profound scholarship, we allot but two years to the course. The young men who have left us have been very useful, and the class now in hand will bear comparison with any body of men living.

I could not, while possessing any self-respect, prepare your son for Dr Angus; but I shall be delighted to be of any other service to him.

Yours most truly,

C. H. SPURGEON

[*An Enquiring Candidate*]

Clapham
Mar. 21st/63

My dear Sir,

The next occasion for receiving students will be in September next, but as there are very many applications I cannot absolutely promise to receive you *then*, but you might not get your turn until Christmas. This I mention in order that you may apply elsewhere if time should be an object.

Meanwhile I should be glad of a little more evidence as to your preaching powers. Could you not send me some notes of sermons, or some essays, or far better, I should prefer the testimony of one or two more persons of judicious character. Not that I distrust Mr Walter's judgment but a few other witnesses will confirm the matter.

Press forward,

Yours truly,

C. H. SPURGEON

[*An Enquiring Candidate*]

Metropolitan Tabernacle
Newington
July 18, 1864

My dear Sir,

Your papers are all I could wish and you are free to join us on September 5th.

One thing however let me suggest – you seem to have already so good an education that I fear you will not find our College course high enough in its range. If this also strikes you, do not think you will hurt my feelings but apply at once to some other College.

It is only in classics that I fear this – for we shall not trouble you with any more Latin if you read 6 book of Virgil.[1]

I don't see the use of more. We aim rather at preaching than classical learning.

Yours very truly,

C. H. SPURGEON

[1] The reference is to Book VI of *The Aeneid* by the Roman author Virgil.

[*An Enquiring Candidate*]

Nightingale Lane
Clapham
Sept. 12–1874

Dear Sir,

I would call your attention to the fact that the two signatures to your schedule appear to be written in the same hand, and one of them is *Mr Dooley* which is not a signature at all. Please send me the addresses of these two persons, for I do not find the name of M. Pritchard among Baptist ministers, nor is *Latimer Street South* mentioned in our hand-book.

You have sent me no testimonials whatever and therefore I cannot judge your case.

Yours truly,
C. H. SPURGEON

[*J. L. Keys*]

Menton
Thursday

Dear Keys,

Has the Conference[1] been arranged for? What is done and what is left to me? I can now see to it if not too late. The

---

[1]In 1865 Spurgeon had originated a Conference of the Pastors' College to which all pastors trained in the College were invited. This annual occasion became a major means of unity between the men of the Pastors' College Association. In addition to the preparation of addresses which he often gave at the Conference (twelve of which are printed in *An All-Round Ministry*, Banner of Truth Trust 1960 and currently remaining in print), Spurgeon had the burden of arranging a well-balanced programme each year – not an easy undertaking as this letter shows. This letter shows that Keys did more than editorial work for Spurgeon (see above p. 88).

men mentioned in your list are nearly all too weak: we must have some stronger brethren. The *subjects* strike me as utter rubbish; not likely to minister to anybody's edification. See my brother about whole matter. Better to postpone till summer rather than have a poor affair.

Yours heartily,
C. H. S.

[*A Colleague*]

Nightingale Lane
Balham, Surrey
Oct. 30, 1879

Dear Friend,

It is very difficult to adapt a College to several objects. Mr Guinness goes in for foreigners and missionaries and whoever may come he is ready: but one such among us would put *us* out of gear, and would hardly benefit *him*.

I am going abroad and shall leave the matter with my brother[1] to do just as he judges best – but I hardly think that we can do much for the gentleman. The case seems to be deeply interesting but you will yourself be better able to judge after seeing him. To your judgment I should greatly defer in any case.

Yours ever heartily,
C. H. SPURGEON

[1]James Archer Spurgeon was Vice-President of the College. This letter was probably written to David Gracey, a tutor who became Rogers' successor as Principal.

[*Members of the Pastors' College Association*]

Nightingale Lane
Balham, Surrey
June 12, 1880

My Dear Friend,

It was agreed upon at the Conference that we should all try to set apart Monday, June 21 as a day of special prayer.

It is my part lovingly to bring to your minds this brotherly covenant, and to express the desire that you may be able to carry it out, and that the Holy Spirit may cause the springs of supplication to flow very freely.

Permit me to send herewith my hearty love in the Lord. We are bound together by living bonds of love, and my prayers rise to heaven for *your* prosperity in Christ. I beseech you pray for *me* when you have THE KING'S ear.

Yours in the Lord Jesus,
C. H. SPURGEON

[*A Colleague*]

Westwood
Beulah Hill
Upper Norwood
Aug. 24, 1880

Dear Friend,

Mr Baskerville is reported to me as a young man of such temper that he is not liked where he has resided and it is feared will not make a suitable person to be connected with respectable families as a Pastor. Will you please report to me what he is as a student, for if not rather remarkably gifted I shall dismiss him. If he is a really good fellow you might talk with him upon the fact that he has conciliated no one, but every one of our lodging-house people who have tried him have been glad to be rid of him.

Mr Billington my brother wants to be *engineer* of the steamer on the Congo; but he thinks he should be a missionary. I wish he had so much grace as to go anyhow. Brother thinks he will be a poor missionary, but beginning as engineer would soon develop and become up to the mark. What do you think? Please advise me.

Tell the men I hope to take the chair on Friday and have a say.

Yours ever heartily,
C. H. SPURGEON

[*Members of the Pastors' College Association*]

Westwood
Beulah Hill
Upper Norwood
June 11, 1881

Dear Friend,

At the College Conference we agreed to set apart Monday, June 20, for a day of prayer. Allow me to beg of you to join the brotherhood in this special supplication. Anything which leads to more prayer is good, and when this also promotes holy brotherhood it is better still.

We need times of refreshing, both at home and abroad. The enemies of the gospel are exceedingly busy and crafty, and we can only meet them by power from on high. The needs of our nation grow upon us, and only One can multiply our loaves and fishes so as to feed the multitude. We ourselves being compassed with infirmities need to be daily girt with fresh strength; and our churches being made up of imperfect men and women can only be kept in healthy, united action by the Spirit of our God.

Brethren, all these are reasons for incessant, importunate prayer. If you could hold several short meetings at different homes, say at 6 or 9, or noon, or at eventide, it would be well. We should oftener have larger meetings if we altered the hours according to the season of the year and the occupation of the people.

Our many brethren abroad all wish to be remembered in our prayers; so also do the sick of our college army; and so above all others does

> Your affectionate brother in the Lord,
> C. H. SPURGEON

[*Rev W. Y. Fullerton*]

> Menton
> Jan. 15, 1884

Dear Mr Fullerton,

I am in such a position that I must even drive a willing horse beyond reason. I want a paper from you for the Conference.

I have been very ill; I am ill still; can barely sit up. Yet this Conference must be arranged, and I write therefore importunately. Do not deny me. I grant it is too bad, etc. – Grant much more, – I am thoughtless, cruel, tyrannical, – all that is bad.

Still, I beg you to say 'Yes'. Some holy spiritual subject. Just handled in your own way.

I groan to see a devout, pleading, spiritual convocation.

You can help towards this as few can. I must be awfully despotic and say *you must*.

God bless you in Leicester. Best love to Smith and yourself. Oh, that the place may be saved! If any in it love the old truth, may God, our Lord, compel them to come out like men.

Yours heartily,
C. H. SPURGEON

[*An Enquiring Married Candidate*]

Westwood
Beulah Hill
Upper Norwood
July 30, 1884

Dear Sir,

Are you still anxious to come to College? My trouble is about your wife and family. Should you not remain as you are? It would only be possible for me to allow you 30/– per week, and rent is high in this place. I fear it would be a sad pinch for the family.

Still you may come in Sep. 1 if you think it wise.

Yours heartily,
C. H. SPURGEON

[*An Accepted Candidate*]

Westwood
Beulah Hill
Upper Norwood
May, 1885

Dear Sir,

I have read your answers and testimonials, and I hope I am doing right when I say – *Come to College on Sep. 1.* I trust the Lord has indeed called you to the ministry and given you the needed gifts and graces, and I pray that he may now anoint you afresh with his Spirit.

During the first session you must regard yourself as specially under trial, for when I have used my best judgment I am apt to be mistaken, and this is soon made evident when the brother gets to his studies. I trust your future career will prove that we have not made a mistake.

Further directions can be had nearer the time from Mr Page. I should like you to have a rest before September that you may enter College in a fresh and vigorous mental and bodily condition.

Pray much for yourself, and for

Yours heartily,
C. H. SPURGEON

[*Members of the Pastors' College Association*]

Metropolitan Tabernacle
Newington, S.E.
March 4, 1887

My dear Friend,

As the time for the College Conference draws nigh I am full of anxiety, and I would desire to let that anxiety condense into prayer. Please join me in that prayer.

Our sole desire is the glory of God, and this would be greatly promoted if we all made a distinct advance in the Divine life: this may be produced by the Holy Spirit through our communion with each other and the Lord. Let us bow low before the throne for this, and take hold upon the promises with a mighty faith.

It is comparatively a small matter to all but myself; but I hunger to be with you all the day every day. We love each other in the Lord, and yet see so little of each other that I am bitterly disappointed if taken from you by pain. Brother, pray that we may look each other in the face, and may together behold our Lord. Would you do me the great service to set apart a little time privately to seek an unusual blessing? and it would be a great gain if in addition you could lead your Church to pray with us. I pine for a heavenly shower to saturate us all.

Please answer the letters of secretaries promptly. This is a huge business: ease us all you can.

Your loving friend,
C. H. SPURGEON

[*An Accepted Candidate*]

Westwood
Beulah Hill
Upper Norwood
May 20, 1889

Dear Sir,

Come to college August 6, and may the Lord prove that this is according to His mind. Come to work hard, and to pray harder. May you be a willing plodder and a great soul-winner.

Yours very truly,
C. H. SPURGEON

[*Members of the Pastors' College Association*]

Metropolitan Tabernacle,
Newington
S.E.
Mar. 10, 1890

My Dear Brother,

The approach of another Conference warns us of the rapid flight of time, and calls for great searchings of heart in looking back. My business just now is to look forward; and I do so by a happy anticipation of a joyful gathering, and next by a heart-fetched prayer that it may be a hallowed, heavenly season.

Brethren will come together seeking to be cheered, encouraged, quickened. My soul prays continually that they may not be disappointed. We dare not rely upon the occasion, the brotherhood, the *esprit de corps*, or anything which is of ourselves. Our help must come from above. We shall simply waste time unless we meet together in the atmosphere of eternity, covered with the wings of the Spirit, and made one in the life of Christ. I beseech you, strive together with me in your prayers that we may have the largest blessings we are able to receive, and that we may be enlarged to receive even more.

Our hope is that brief addresses and short prayers will prove more fruitful than longer discourses might have been. If every brother who speaks is filled with the Spirit of God, we shall have no profitless talk; and if all who are coming would aim to be so filled, we should have a wealth of spiritual profiting.

Personally I beg your prayers. There is much to wear away the soul just now, and we need that text to be true in our experience 'he restoreth my soul'. I know that I need the visitation of the Lord to refresh my spirit. Do we not each one need it? What if we should each one get it? How good for ourselves, for our churches, our hearers! Oh that the Lord may come very near us, and clothe us with power from on high!

My brother, if you have been of the Conference for years, I may say that we may not meet many times more; let us avail ourselves of every occasion, and use it to the full.

If you are a newer comer, I would beg you to drop more and more into the unity of our fraternal unity, and be sure to attend the annual feast.

Do be so good as to answer our secretaries at once. It is a great work to arrange and carry through this Conference. Please aid us by your promptness.

> Yours most lovingly,
> C. H. SPURGEON

[*A Parent*]

> Westwood
> Beulah Hill
> Upper Norwood
> Mar. 14, 1891

Dear Sir,

We only receive men in August and therefore those applying have to wait till the time for taking account of the whole company of applicants.

You do not give me your own estimate of your son's abilities. His character is all we could desire. I do not, however, think that he will be wise to leave his calling. At the end of the term there may be no vacant pastorate, and if he should get one, it is a position of severe trial and usually of scanty means. He can do as much good probably in his present position as he will ever do.

I would like to set before him the darker side of the picture, that he may 'count the cost'.

The testimonies which I have received are not sufficient to convince me of his call to the ministry, and if [I] have to give an answer now, it must be in the negative. I should be very sorry for that to be taken as a sign from the Lord, for my judgment is a very fallible one, and the matter which I have before me to decide by is far too slender.

Yours very heartily,

C. H. SPURGEON

Westwood
Beulah Hill
Upper Norwood
Mar. 18, 1891

Dear Mr Tooke,

Your case is one upon which I cannot decide favourably. I fear you are not likely to make a thoroughly efficient minister. I can only judge by the testimonials you have sent me, and the few enquiries I can make.

In your present calling you can serve the Lord and maintain yourself, but I would not have you become, as many are, a charge upon a people who have to put up with you. There are too many in these days who are poorly paid because they poorly preach. Of course there are real heroes who are as efficient as they are poor; but I would not increase the army of the in-efficients.

I would counsel you to go on as you are, and do all you can for our Lord. I must decline your application.

Yours very truly,

C. H. SPURGEON

7: ASPECTS OF WORK AT THE METROPOLITAN TABERNACLE

[*John T. Dunn*[1]]

Nightingale Lane
Clapham
Sept. 2

Dear Mr Dunn,

Please see into Beddow's case. He left his wife and family at Belper and for a time sent them 5/- a week, while he was having a decent salary as an evangelist. Even this he failed to send and I was applied to about it; I recommended that she should apply to the parish.

He now denies this as you see; but if you draw him out you will see it is true. Get from him his wife's address.

I think there is something queer about his leaving his last place. Find out all you can. He is so dirty etc. that he has long disgraced the College, and I shall be glad to wash my hands of him. Mrs Beddow I suspect can a tale unfold.

Yours very truly,

C. H. SPURGEON

[1]Dunn joined the New Park Street congregation in 1859 when he was a London City Missionary. He was appointed an elder in 1861 and a few years later became Church Secretary and Spurgeon's assistant, with special responsibility for pastoral visitation. Correspondence with Dunn shows something of the mundane matters with which Spurgeon often had to deal.

As other letters in this book partly reveal, the work at the Tabernacle was far wider and demanding than is indicated by the short selection of material in this chapter.

[*The Church in the Tabernacle*]

Menton
February 28 [1878]

Beloved Friends,

I rejoice to think that my return to you is now a matter of a few days, and that I have every prospect, if the Lord will, of returning with health established and mind restored. Perhaps never before have I been brought so low in spirit, and assuredly never more graciously restored. May the Lord sanctify both the trial and the recovery, so that I may be the fitter instrument, in His hand, to promote His glory and your highest good. The last fortnight of additional rest was wisely ordained by a higher hand than that of the good deacons who suggested it to me, for without it I should not have had space to pass through an attack of pain which has just swept over me, and left me improved by its violence. The last few days will, I feel, be the best of the whole, when I shall not have to be thoughtful of recovery, but altogether restful. Good news from the Tabernacle continues to be as cold water to a thirsty soul. You have had great times of refreshing; may their influence abide with you. We must not go to sleep on my return, nor at any other time, but steadily labour on and watch for souls. Spurts are very helpful, but to keep up the pace at a high regular figure is the most important thing. Even an invalid can make a great exertion when some remarkable occasion excites him to do so; but consistent, unwearied effort belongs only to those who have stamina and inward force. May our whole church prove itself to be strong in the Lord and in the power of His might by unceasingly carrying on its work of faith and labour of love. In these days we are regarded as Puritanical and old-fashioned, and this, I trust, we shall never be ashamed of, but wear it as an ornament. The old orthodox faith is to us no outward creed of past ages, but a thing of power. In the name of the Lord, who by that faith is honoured, we press forward to proclaim again and again the doctrines of the grace of God, the efficacy of the blood of the Divine Substitute, and the power of the Eternal Spirit. And we feel assured that whoever may oppose, the omnipotent Gospel will prevail. The multitudes are hungering for that old-fashioned bread whereof their fathers fed; and too many preachers now give them newly-carved stones, and bid them admire the skill of the modern sculptors. We mean to continue the distribution of bread, and the stone-cutters will meet with no competition from us in their favourite amusement. But, brethren, only a living church – holy, prayerful, active – can make the old truths victorious. Linked with the mass of mere profession, it will perform no exploits. To you and to me there is a growing call for greater spirituality and more Divine power, for the work before us increases in difficulty. The Lord be with you all. So prays yours lovingly,

C. H. SPURGEON

Westwood
Beulah Hill
Upper Norwood
May 16, 1882

Dear Mr Dunn,

My brother tells me you purpose 3 weeks for Mr Booth. I do not believe we could keep it up that time successfully and I think one Sunday evening, the second in the month, and one week of meetings will be all that it will be wise to hold. There is such a displacing of other things, and so much expense connected with it that we must not have a failure, and I am sure three weeks would be a failure for the thing would flag.

This is not our chief work either, and can only be carried on in due subordination to our usual engagements. We must not weary our brethren whom we hope to win.

Yours ever heartily,

C. H. SPURGEON

[*To all the Tabernacle Sabbath School following Spurgeon's 50th birthday*]

Westwood
Beulah Hill
Upper Norwood
June 21, 1884

Dear Mr Pearce,

I salute you as the Captain of the Host below stairs and in the college. Peace be to you, and to all your helpers. Brethren and sisters beloved, I value your affection above rubies, and I breathe my prayers to heaven that all covenant blessings may be yours.

Dear young ones who are saved, the Lord keep you, and ripen your graces, and gladden your hearts.

Dear boys and girls, not yet saved, the silver trumpets of Jubilee invite you to come to Jesus today. The sooner you trust the Lord Jesus the sooner you will be happy, safe, and holy. Believe in him and live. You will be worthy men and women if you become believing children. Why not? Jesus is ready to receive you.

May the school be a model to all England of true graciousness. You have the dearest superintendent that ever lived, and some of the choicest teachers yet on earth. Many dear children among you love the Lord; may all do so at once, for HE deserves it.

You have all united to make me glad. The Lord God Almighty bless you all at this hour.

> Your loving Pastor,
> C. H. SPURGEON

[*The Sabbath School Superintendent*]

> Westwood
> Jan. 20, 1888

Dear Friend,

Say Mar. 12 as the Ladies' Benevolent is on the 5th. The Lord be with you and all the teachers. I love you all for Jesus' sake. Your holy unity in the truth is a well-spring of comfort to my heart. I thank you ten thousand times for your faithfulness to our Lord, to His Word, and to me, His servant. It is a joy to think of the Sabbath School, and its valued Superintendent, and soul-winning teachers. I invoke upon you all the infinite blessing of God.

> Yours in Jesus for ever,
> C. H. SPURGEON

[*The Men's Bible Class*]

Westwood
Beulah Hill
Upper Norwood
July 5, 1886

Dear Brethren,

You know that my heart ever beats true to the Class, and its well-beloved leader. If my knees would but prove as strong as my affections. I should be with you at a bound; but, alas, the spirit is willing, but the legs are weakness itself.

Young men, work for the Lord while you can. It would greatly embitter my seasons of painful retirement if I could accuse myself with having wasted the time of my health and strength. When I can work, I pack a mass into small compass because I am so painfully aware that days and weeks may come wherein I cannot work.

The more I suffer the more I cling to the gospel. *It is true*, and the fires only burn it into clearer certainty to my soul. I have lived on the gospel, and I can die on it. Never question it.

Go on to win other souls. It is the only thing worth living for. God is much glorified by conversions, and therefore this should be the great object of life.

Be earnest, be prayerful, be united. Study the Word, and practise it. Live *on* Christ, and live *for* Him. My best blessing, and heartiest love be with you and Mr Dunn.[1]

Yours heartily,
C. H. SPURGEON

[1]John Dunn was President of the Men's Bible Class for twenty years.

Westwood
Beulah Hill
Upper Norwood
188[?]

Dear Mr Dunn,

Come on Saturday morning and see into the case of *Sarah Marsh* deceased at the house of J. Weller as by enclosed bill. She claimed to be a member with us, and this is the point. Is she? She is an aged woman with husband. Both poor; back in rent. She has had fits and died in one.

If really a member give such help as you think wise. If you are round here at about 1 or 1.30 there will be dinner for you.

Yours truly,
C. H. SPURGEON

Westwood
Beulah Hill
Upper Norwood
Jan. 16, 1885

Dear Mr Dunn,

I helped Mrs Withers last year, but I have a very low opinion of her.

We can have nothing to do with her taking a house. She left Mr Stiff's house in a way which I did not admire. Ask him.

We cannot support persons who are not members with us. She must apply to her own church.

I would like you at any rate to enquire into her character from others. She talks like a parrot with his tail on fire. She has applied to Mr Douglas to join Solon Road, but he told me he had a question, and I recommended him to be cautious, which is also my counsel to you.

Dear Friend, look well to the flock in my absence, and the Lord be with you.

> Yours truly,
> C. H. SPURGEON

> Westwood
> Beulah Hill,
> Upper Norwood
> June 5, 1891

Dear Mr Dunn,

This is a puzzling case, for the young man questioned my brother and all the elders, and was rude to the last degree.

Elvin thinks him a mass of conceit, and I fear he is *that*. Nevertheless I see no good in stopping *now*. It would be like playing the fool. As my brother is satisfied, I am.

My judgment is that the blame of his getting so far is ours, and he must now be received. If he does not attend, the fault will be his own, and we can drop him.

He seeks to get into the College, and I don't think he will.

Let it be known through the papers that I hope to preach on Sunday morning.

Keep well.

> Yours heartily,
> C. H. SPURGEON

8: FRAGMENTS:
SOME OF THE SHORTEST
LETTERS

ON HIS PUBLISHERS' 'RETIREMENT'

[1866]

Dear Mr Passmore,[1]

Have you retired from business? For, if not, I should be glad of proofs for the month of November of a book entitled *Morning by Morning* which, unless my memory fails me, you began to print. I was to have had some matter on Monday; and it is now Wednesday. Please jog the friend who has taken your business, and tell him that YOU always were the very soul of punctuality, and that he must imitate you.

I send a piece for October 31, for I can't find any proof for that date. Please let the gentleman who has taken your business have it soon.

Yours ever truly,

C. H. SPURGEON

P.S. Has Mr Alabaster retired, too? I congratulate you both, and hope the new firm will do as well. What is the name? I'll make a guess, – MESSRS. QUICK AND SPEEDY.

[1]From the outset of his ministry in London, Joseph Passmore and James Alabaster had been Spurgeon's publishers and he became so attached to them that, he writes, 'I had no wish to have any other publishers as long as I lived'. His hopes, expressed to Passmore in a letter of May 17, 1854, were to be abundantly fulfilled: 'We have, I trust, just commenced a new era; and, by God's blessing, we will strive to make it a glorious one to our Church.' Passmore and Alabaster published his sermons, *The Sword and the Trowel*, and all his other publications. The above letter is, of course, an example of Spurgeon's humour.

ON THE GIFT OF A TABLE[1]

Clapham
Nov. 16, '71

Dear Mr Goldston,

Warranty of Table.

This is to certify that the table this day sent to Mr Goldston has never been known to turn, twist, dance, fly up into the air or otherwise misbehave. It has not been addicted to convivial habits and has never been known to be on a roar. As a most studious piece of furniture it is sent to a studious man with the kind regards of

C. H. SPURGEON

AMERICAN NEWSPAPERS CORRECTED

Clapham
London
July 6, 1876

Gentlemen,

I cannot imagine how such a paragraph should appear in your papers, except by deliberate invention of a hard-up Editor, for I never had any idea of leaving home for America for some time to come. As I said to you before, if I could come, I am not a lecturer, nor would I receive money for preaching.

Yours truly,
C. H. SPURGEON

[1]This humorous letter to a friend accompanied the gift of the study table which Spurgeon had used for the first fifteen years of his ministry in London.

A SISTER'S PROBLEM

> Westwood
> Beulah Valley
> Nov. 9, 1880

Dear Sister,[1]

I don't know what I can say to prove that you are my sister. Perhaps your certificate of Birth would settle it – but then, ladies don't like their age to be known.

I oh! let the gossips talk till they have done – for they can't alter the undoubted fact that I am

> Your loving brother,
> C. H. S.

SMOKING[2]

Dear ———,

I cultivate my flowers and burn my weeds.

> Yours truly,
> C. H. SPURGEON

[1]Which one of Spurgeon's six sisters is addressed in this letter is not recorded.

[2]This reply was sent to a gentleman who wrote to Spurgeon saying he 'had heard he smoked, and could not believe it true'. For Spurgeon's fuller defence of smoking see *Life and Work of C. H. Spurgeon*, G. H. Pike, vol. 5, p. 139, where he complains of 'a Pharisaic system which adds to the commands of God the precepts of men'. But Spurgeon was unaware of the effects of nicotine upon health.

GRATITUDE

Westwood
Beulah Hill
Upper Norwood
June 19, 1883

Dear Friend,

Your princely note with cheque for £100 has come to me before breakfast on my birthday. *God bless you.* I am deeply grateful for the orphans' sake. To you may there be constant joy and peace 'till the day break and the shadows flee away'.

Yours gratefully,
C. H. SPURGEON

ON THE LOAN OF BOOKS

Westwood
Beulah Hill
Upper Norwood, S.E.
Oct. 9, 1886

Dear Mr McAusland,

I do not like being security for a man that he will return books, for no ordinary mortals ever do so. Please hold me harmless by scrupulously returning each vol. intact and with promptness. I don't like it, but I have done it *for you*. God bless you.

Yours truly,
C. H. SPURGEON

ENCOURAGEMENT TO A SUNDAY-SCHOOL TEACHER

Westwood
Beulah Hill
Upper Norwood
May 16, 1888

Dear Friend,

The Lord bless you in the work of your hands, and soon set you free.

I hope the liver will wake up. I am in seas of trouble, but the Lord High Admiral is on board.

I will aid you as to books for Sunday School, and in any other way you desire.

Yours very lovingly,
C. H. SPURGEON

9: ON QUESTIONS OF CHRISTIAN DOCTRINE AND PRACTICE

FINAL PERSEVERANCE

Westwood
March 15, 1887

Dear Friend,

As to Hebrews, I have always taught that if the Divine life could entirely *die out* there would be no second quickening. We can be born again, but not again and again. If the salt could lose its savour, it would be a hopeless case. From which I argue that, as no man is in a hopeless case, no man has utterly lost the life of God after once receiving it.

The wilful return to sin would be fatal.

In each passage quoted the evil supposed is also denied. See Heb. vi. 9; Heb. x. 39.

One great means of securing final perseverance is the knowledge that we cannot go in and out of Christ at pleasure: if we could utterly quit Him, there could be no possibility of renewal. Heb. vi. 4. Therefore we are bound to hold on even to the end.

My wonder is how, in the teeth of these texts, Arminians believe men to lose the Divine life and receive it again. No words can be clearer than those which describe this as impossible.

I have sent a catalogue with sermons marked which may help you.

Write me whenever you like, only excuse me if I am brief.

Yours heartily,
C. H. SPURGEON

INFANT SALVATION

Newington, S.E.
June 12, 1869

Dear Sir,

I have never, at any time in my life, said, believed, or imagined that any infant, under any circumstances, would be cast into hell. I have always believed in the salvation of all infants, and I intensely detest the opinions which your opponent dared to attribute to me. I do not believe that, on this earth, there is a single professing Christian holding the damnation of infants; or, if there be, he must be insane, or utterly ignorant of Christianity. I am obliged by this opportunity of denying the calumny, although the author of it will probably find no difficulty in inventing some other fiction to be affirmed as unblushingly as the present one. He who doubts God's Word is naturally much at home in slandering the Lord's servants.

Yours truly,
C. H. SPURGEON

ERROR AND CHURCH MEMBERSHIP

Clapham
July 20

Sir,

I am sorry that Mr —— stultifies his own convictions, and distresses others, by remaining with a church whose testimony is diametrically opposed to his opinions. It seems to me that a Christian man is bound to unite with a church where he may consistently hold and promulgate his views; but he has no excuse if he remains with a people to whom his views are obnoxious, and where his agitation of his opinions tends to create strife and division. We, as a church at the Tabernacle, cultivate fellowship with all the churches of our Lord, although differing in many respects from some of them; but, within our own membership, we have a basis of agreement in doctrine and practice, and where a member differs from it, it is his duty to remove to some other community where his views are held, or else he must expect us to withdraw from him. I have taken no further action in the case of Mr —— than to request him to find a more congenial fellowship; but if he does not do so, our discipline must take its usual course. No honest man can be a member of the church meeting at the Tabernacle, and hold annihilationist views, for now and in all time past we have borne testimony to the generally-received doctrine.

Yours truly,
C. H. SPURGEON

PRESERVING HARMONY OF BELIEF IN CHURCHES

Benmore [Scotland],
July 22, 1880

Dear Sir,

It is not easy to advise upon a particular case by giving general rules, but my experience has taught me the unwisdom of receiving into a mere nucleus a person or persons of singular views. In addition to the danger incurred internally there is the liability of the erroneous opinion being imputed to the whole body and its being stigmatised accordingly. This we would readily bear for truth's sake but ought not wilfully to incur by a questionable comprehensiveness.

You do not expect me to enter into the question under debate. It seems clear enough to me, however, that if punishment is to last for ever so must those who endure it. To live and to exist are not synonymous terms, neither does to die convey to my mind the idea of non-existence. But the point is – can there be *useful* union when this point is raised and I fear not.

I am for keeping membership of our churches strict and the communion free to all members of churches; but if churches are corrupt I should feel that ground to be untenable. I am not able to guide you in the point. May the Lord direct you.

Yours heartily,
C. H. SPURGEON

ABSTINENCE FROM ALCOHOL[1]

March 15, 1882

Dear Friends,

I am exceedingly sorry to be absent from this first meeting to form the Tabernacle Total Abstinence Society. The worse of it is, that my head is so out of order that I cannot even dictate a proper letter. I can only say, 'Try

[1]In a letter to a Mr Mayers, March 4, 1882, Spurgeon says: 'I have no wine-glasses in the house, so that all who come here must go without, especially as there is no alcohol on the premises . . .' He had become an abstainer during the course of his ministry but he did not make it an issue: 'I have been urged to preach on teetotalism but I lay the axe at the root of the tree'. On this subject see *Personal Reminiscences of C. H. Spurgeon*, W. Williams, pp. 39–40.

and do all the better because I am away.' If the leader is shot down, and his legs are broken, the soldiers must give an extra hurrah, and rush on the enemy. I sincerely believe that, next to the preaching of the gospel, the most necessary thing to be done in England is to induce our people to become total abstainers. I hope this Society will do something when it is started. I don't want you to wear a lot of peacocks' feathers and putty medals, nor to be always trying to convert the moderate drinkers, but to go in for winning the real drunkards, and bringing the poor enslaved creatures to the feet of Jesus, who can give them liberty. I wish I could say ever so many good things, but I cannot, and so will remain,

> Yours teetotally,
> C. H. SPURGEON

THE STATE AND MARRIAGE

> Westwood
> April 9, 1881

Dear Friend,

I regard marriage as a civil contract, which ought to be made before a magistrate or a registrar. I should be glad to be rid of marrying and burying altogether as religious matters, save only where there is a sincere desire for the Divine blessing or consolation. In these cases, let the minister hold a service at the house or the meeting-house; but do not make him a State official to register marriages, and to be held responsible for all the intricacies of marriage law.

I hope Mr Briggs' proposal will never pass, or anything like it. If it did, I could only refuse to marry anybody, for I will not become a registrar. I altogether agree with the reported action of the Liberation Society, and wish for the time when all marriages shall be at the registrar's office, and then the godly can have such religious service afterwards as they wish.[1]

> Yours ever heartily,
> C. H. SPURGEON

VIVISECTION

> Westwood
> July 25, 1881

Dear Sir,

I am unable to attend your garden meeting. I wish evermore the utmost success to all protests against the inhuman practice of vivisection. It does not bear to be thought of. How it must excite the righteous indignation of the all-merciful Creator! It is singularly sad that there should need to be an agitation on such a question; for one would think that the least-enlightened conscience would perceive the evil of such cruelty, and that the most-hardened heart would retain sufficient humanity to revolt against it.

> Yours truly,
> C. H. SPURGEON

[1] Spurgeon was not, however, envisaging a time when his nation would cast off the light of Scripture upon marriage.

MOODY AND SANKEY IN LONDON
[*Mr Ben Nicholson*]

Westwood
April 1, 1882

Dear Friend,

I am the earnest friend and helper of all who preach the Gospel of Jesus; yet I deem it no unfriendly thing to speak the truth, and what I wrote in 1876 I have never seen any reason to alter. Messrs. Moody and Sankey are two blessed men of God, and if their converts on that occasion vanished it was no fault of theirs, neither would I have had them refrain for an hour – far from it.[1]

The movement in London had comparatively no link with the Churches, and fostered a rival spirit, and hence it did not bring a permanent blessing of increase to the Churches. Still it brought a great blessing to the Church Universal, and revived and encouraged us all.

I would warn Churches against *trusting* in spasmodic effort, but at the same time against refusing such special help as the Lord puts in their way. There is a medium.

In any case I am not *against* evangelistic effort, but heartily its advocate.

Yours very truly and gratefully,

C. H. SPURGEON

[1]'He greatly admired Mr Moody and his work,' writes William Williams (*Personal Reminiscences*, p. 56), though he was ready to criticise some of the changes in evangelism which became popular following the campaigns of the two Americans. Spurgeon never used a public appeal for would-be converts to 'come to the front'. See *The Forgotten Spurgeon*, Iain H. Murray, Banner of Truth Trust, 1966.

ON PUBLIC BAPTISMS

Westwood
May 13, 1885

Dear Mr Soper,

I was not present at Sheepwash; and, consequently, can form no opinion as to the behaviour of the villagers after the baptism was over; but I remember that the same things were said, more than thirty years ago, of our public baptisms in Cambridgeshire, and I daresay there is as much truth in the representations now made as in those of the older time.

Those who did not wish to see so much of baptism imagined evils which existed mainly in their fears.

Baptism in the open river is so Scriptural, and, withal, such a public testimony, that I hope our friends will never abandon it. The reproach is to be bravely borne; for, if you hide away in the meeting-house, it will follow you there. We are most numerous where the ordinance is most known. Next to the Word of God, a baptising service is the best argument for baptism.

Whenever numbers of people come together, whether for trade, politics, or religion, there will always be loose persons to dishonour the occasion; but we are not therefore to abstain from such gatherings. Such an inference would be absurd.

God bless and prosper you!

Yours heartily,
C. H. SPURGEON

EVOLUTION

Westwood
Feb. 8, 1887

Dear Sir,

Thanks for your most excellent and courteous letter. I have read a good deal on the subject, and have never yet seen a fact, or the tail of a fact, which indicated the rise of one species of animal into another. The theory has been laid down, and facts fished up to support it. I believe it to be a monstrous error in philosophy, which will be a theme for ridicule before another twenty years.

In theology, its influence would be deadly; and this is all I care about. On the scientific matter, you do well to use your own judgment.

The Lord bless you, and lead you into *His* truth more and more!

Yours heartily,

C. H. SPURGEON

SHOULD A CALL TO AN ARMINIAN CHURCH BE ACCEPTED?

Westwood
Beulah Hill
Upper Norwood
Mar. 1, 1889

Dear Mr Mills,

The Derby friends wrote me and I most heartily recommended *you* to them; but now you puzzle me. I do not know these brethren well enough to form a judgment upon the matter.

As a rule, I do not see how we who are Calvinistic can become pastors of avowedly Arminian churches; but if these good people know our views and desire our preaching, I could not draw a hard and fast line.

There is a vital difference between us and the Down-Graders, but there is a clear evangelistic platform upon which we can stand with G.B's.[1]

Cliffordism[2] will ruin the General Baptists if generally adopted and many of them see it. Do not in the least compromise yourself but do not stop for mere names.

The Lord direct you, for I cannot. Hope to see you soon. I always love you.

Yours most heartily,
C. H. SPURGEON

'CATCHING FLEAS'

Dear Friend,
You amuse me with your question about the Supper. It certainly was not instituted on the Lord's Day, and if we are to raise such old legal niceties, by all means let us always imitate the Lord Himself, and never commune except on a Thursday.

You are too good and large-hearted a man to let such questions bother you. It reminds me of catching fleas.

Yours truly,
C. H. SPURGEON

[1]The distinction here is, of course, between the differences which exist between evangelical Christians and those between them and the liberal 'Down-Graders' who rejected such fundamental truths as the authority of Scripture, the wrath of God against sin and the atoning work of the Son of God. Among the Nonconformist denominations General Baptists and Methodists were commonly Arminian in belief.

[2]John Clifford, Baptist leader who favoured the liberalising of belief.

BRETHREN–*ism*[1]

Westwood
May 9, 1890

Dear Sir,

I cannot say that I have changed my opinion as to Brethren-*ism*; but with many Brethren I have always been on most brotherly terms. I don't think I am bound to answer your questions about individuals. I believe that I was loved by C.S., and that Mr Kelly regards me in the kindest manner; and I return the like to the memory of the first, and to the other who survives. I am, perhaps, better able to sympathise with their separateness *now* than aforetime; but their ideas of the ministry I do not accept.

Yours very truly,

C. H. SPURGEON

[1]In his earlier ministry Spurgeon had often expressed or supported criticism of the Plymouth Brethren movement and especially of its Darbyite section (e.g., *Metropolitan Tabernacle Pulpit*, 1862, pp. 195–96, 202–3; *The Sword and the Trowel*, 1865, pp. 282–87; *The Sword and Trowel*, 1867, p. 32 etc). One of his main criticisms, namely that their view of eldership undermined the gospel ministry, was abiding as this letter shows. 'The outcry against the "one man ministry" cometh not of God.'

10: ILLNESS AND LETTERS FROM MENTON

[Mrs Susannah Spurgeon[1]]

My own dear Sufferer,   [1869]

I am pained indeed to learn, from T——'s kind note, that you are still in so sad a condition! Oh, may the ever-merciful God be pleased to give you ease!

I have been quite a long round to-day, if a 'round' can be 'long'. First, to Finsbury, to buy the wardrobe, – a beauty. I hope you will live long to hang your garments in it, every thread of them precious to me for your dear sake. Next, to Hewlett's, for a chandelier for the dining- room. Found one quite to my taste and yours. Then, to Negretti & Zambra's, to buy a barometer for my very own fancy, for I have promised to treat myself to one. On the road, I obtained the Presburg biscuits, and within their box I send this note, hoping it may reach you the more quickly. They are sweetened with my love and prayers.

The bedroom will look well with the wardrobe in it; at least, so I hope. It is well made; and, I believe, as nearly as I could tell, precisely all you wished for. Joe (Mr Passmore gave this handsome present) is very good,

---

[1] At this time, when they were about to move into a new home, Mrs Spurgeon was in Brighton where she underwent surgery. Her health never seems to have fully recovered and William Williams, who often visited their home from about the mid-1870's, says: 'Mrs Spurgeon suffered greatly during all the years I visited the home . . . the patient and even exultant resignation of her spirit to the will of God' deeply touched him. *Personal Reminiscences*, p. 66.

and should have a wee note whenever darling feels she could write it without too much fatigue; – but not yet. I bought also a table for you in case you should have to keep your bed. It rises and falls by a screw, and also winds sideways, so as to go over the bed, and then it has a flap for a book or paper, so that my dear one may read or write in comfort while lying down. I could not resist the pleasure of making this little gift to my poor suffering wifey, only hoping it might not often be in requisition, but might be a help when there was a needs-be for it. Remember, all I buy, I pay for. I have paid for everything as yet with the earnings of my pen, graciously sent me in time of need. It is my ambition to leave nothing for you to be anxious about. I shall find the money for the curtains, etc., and you will amuse yourself by giving orders for them after your own delightful taste.

I must not write more; and, indeed, matter runs short, except the old, old story of a love which grieves over you, and would fain work a miracle, and raise you up to perfect health. I fear the heat afflicts you. Well did the elder say to John in Patmos, concerning those who are before the throne of God, 'neither shall the sun light on them, nor any heat.'

Yours to love in life, and death, and eternally,

C. H. S.

Nightingale Lane
Clapham
Sept. 8, 1873

Dear Friend,
Gladly would I have been with you long ere this, but I am not able. I am only staggering along under my load and more I cannot attempt without being a suicide.

I own my obligations to you, but have patience with thy poor servant. I wish I were made of iron, but being only dust, and that of the softest sort, I am pretty generally either ill or upon the verge of it. Tell your good people that if I were as able as I am willing I should be with them the moment you ask me. No one has more heartily my sympathy than you have, and it would give me great pleasure to serve you. When you came to London last time you enabled me to have the first night's sleep I had enjoyed for many weeks. I was becoming demented with the sleeplessness of a brain over-wrought. Having tried now a dozen times I am driven to the belief that I cannot do more than my usual work without breaking down altogether.

> With much love and esteem,
> Yours most gratefully,
> C. H. SPURGEON

[*Rev A. G. Brown*]

> Clapham

Loving Brother,

I thank you much for preaching for me, praying for me, and loving me. I am better, but have had a sharp nip. Lucian says, 'I thought a cobra had bitten me, and filled my veins with poison; but it was worse, – *it was gout.*' *That was written from experience, I know.* Yet I bless God for this suffering also, and believe that your prophetic card will be truer than Dr Cumming's[1] vaticinations.

> Yours ever lovingly,
> C. H. S.

[1] A Victorian preacher who specialised in 'prophecy' and in 'the signs of the times'.

[*To my dear Church and People*]

Hotel Meurice
Paris
Friday [March 9, 1877]

My Dearly Beloved Brethren,

You will share in the bitter disappointment which has befallen me, and will sorrow in my sorrow. I never felt better than when I left Menton, where I had really rested and gained refreshment.[1] I hoped to be with you in bodily, mental, and spiritual vigour. On the first day of leaving my warm retreat a fierce wind and sharp frost chilled me to the bone. I travelled home in great pain until I reached this city, and now since Sunday I have been unable to move. Rheumatic pains seemed to paralyse the muscles, and I cannot stand. This is not what I looked for, and is unutterably painful to me. Away from wife and home, I have had to spend sleepless nights in fierce anguish; but I desire publicly to express my gratitude to my heavenly Father for it all. I cannot *see* any good in it, nor perceive the love that ordained it; but I am sure my Lord has done for me the best and kindest thing possible, and so I would say, and do say, Bless the Lord, O my soul.

This will soon be over, and I shall be among you in answer to your loving prayers. My love be with you all in Christ Jesus.

C. H. SPURGEON

[1]Spurgeon first visited Menton in the winter of 1871–2 and by the mid-1870s this resort on the French Riviera, close to the Italian border, had become his favourite retreat. He had spent six weeks there prior to the writing of this letter. The painful and depressing disease of 'gout' had first begun to affect him in December 1869 and, periodically, it became worse so that approximately one third of the last twenty-two years of his ministry was spent out of the Tabernacle pulpit, either suffering, convalescing, or taking precautions against the return of illness. See *C. H. Spurgeon, Autobiography, vol. 2: The Full Harvest*, pp. 193–98, 403–17.

[*A Church Officer at the Tabernacle*]

Menton
Wednesday

Dear Mr ——,

I have a cold upon me, and have had to keep in, but I am much improving through the rest and warmth of this place. I wish you all a merry Christmas. The Lord be with all the deacons and elders in their holy gatherings . . . I trust all will go well. I fear I shall need a week or so more than I at first proposed, since I lost a fortnight by being taken ill. I wish I could be always well, and I have denied myself much to gain it; but I must bow before the Divine will, and do my best. I look up with prayerful faith to our great Father to bless the Church in my absence, and make my absence as little injurious as may be . . . May the Lord bless the preaching, and glorify His name in His own people.

Go and see Mrs ——. If she needs anything, I should be glad to supply it; but you can hardly mention it to her. Please find out in a side way. I hope you and your household are well.

Yours very heartily,
C. H. SPURGEON

[*The Church at the Tabernacle*]

Westwood
Beulah Hill
Upper Norwood
Mar. 12, 1882

Dear Friends,

To my own grievous disappointment my old disorder has come upon me like an armed man and laid me low. I cannot walk or even stand and the pain renders it difficult for me to think consecutively upon any subject. This is a heavy trial to me and all the more so coming as it does when it will cause disappointment to so many who will come tonight to hear me.[1]

I entreat you to pray that this affliction may be greatly sanctified to me, and that it may quickly be removed. I am cheerfully hopeful that it is not so fierce an attack as others which I have suffered and that I shall speedily be among you. Meanwhile to you all I wish joy and to myself PATIENCE.

The Lord be with you.

Your loving Pastor,
C. H. SPURGEON

[*A Medical Adviser*]

Westwood
Beulah Hill
Upper Norwood
May 2, 1882

Dear Sir,

The headache continued to become more and more intense. I took the diminished dose at 10 on Monday, and before 12 I was in a very painful state.

Omitting further medicine I felt better, but in the evening shock returned. Pains in the ears, jaws, and temples flashed continually. I felt strung up, and ready to snap.

I took a dose of Tonga [?] about 12, as I could think of

---

[1] It would appear that this letter was written to be read at the Thursday night prayer meeting – at which Spurgeon normally gave an address.

nothing else. Soon after the pain concentrated on the top of the head, as if I had received a double fracture upon the summit of the skull. I do not understand this. The top of my head feels sore now that the paroxysm is past, and I have a sort of nervous fear of moving about. For the present I would rather leave this powerful medicine.

The leg and foot are better. I can now hobble about, and if the weather would improve, I would soon be out of doors.

Is it only my fancy that my fingers seemed to be twitched about?

Yours truly,

C. H. SPURGEON

[*Rev J. A. Spurgeon*]

Menton
December 2, 1882

My dear Brother,

Love to you and the dear wifie. I am well, and I feel better than I remember to have been for years. Every day I have time for reading, meditation, prayer, etc., and I feel as if my brain boxes were filling up. I keep on accumulating thought from day to day. Once I gathered here a year's materials, and found it a great help all the rest of the year. It is very much so at this time. The Lord is very gracious to me, and I am much alone with Him. So I trust I shall gather that which it will be a joy to sow.

S. has been with me here all the while, nervously broken down; but he is every way better and will do good work yet. He is humble and gracious.

Mr B. is also with us, a very genial, good man. He is very happy with us and we with him. These brethren go off in the morning when the hint is given. I believe I am serving my age by staying here, and gathering matter for future use.

I am so deeply indebted to you for looking into detail at Stockwell, and to your dear wife also. Now we shall go ahead. Mr Carr writes me, singing your praises in a *carmen* of rapture, and the key is not too highly pitched. You are a good brother, indeed.

Please remember me to all souls and all saints at Tabernacle, and to such souls and saints at Croydon as may know me.

Fix time for College recess – say Thursday, December 14, if it seem good.

Yours most lovingly,

C. H. SPURGEON

Menton
Sunday

Dear Mr Dunn,

It is cloudy, cold, and wet here. I am being hardened off. It could not be better done. We see the snow on the hills and yesterday we saw it fall on the mountain summits: it looked like a bridal veil.

I am not well: think I never shall be long together. But I am neither lame in heart or tongue and hope to be in my place on 23rd.

Wickerson will do:– must do. He has gathered the people and it is due to him to have the field. Go with my best blessing; and may the Lord prosper the work.

I send my love to you and Gwillam and Bartlett and all my Enquirer's staff. May we soon be at it.

I feel very timid. My illness leaves one half frightened. I am a poor creature. Pray for me and pray for the Conference.

Yours ever heartily,

C. H. SPURGEON

[*An Elder at the Tabernacle*]

Villa les Grottes
Menton
Jan. 23

Dear Friend,

It is a great pleasure to hear from you, and especially to know that the poor are not forgotten. You will never displease me by being too liberal in disbursing alms for me for I know you do it wisely. I have had sharp pains but I am recovering. Only my back is broken and I need new vertebrae. I feel delighted in the prospect of coming home though this is a dry, bright, sunny, paradisaical place.

Give my love to all the elders, especially the newly married young ones. May the good Lord spare us to each other for many a year and then allow us to get together in heaven. I preached on Sunday from '*your joy no man taketh from you.*'[1] All our brethren know that treasure, – that joy. Let us be as joyful as the angels.

Your loving friend,

C. H. SPURGEON

[1]Other Christian visitors at Menton frequently met with Spurgeon for a morning prayer meeting or for Sunday services.

Hôtel Beau Rivage
Menton
December 15

Dear Friend,

Your kind note has reached me and cheered me. I had eight sunny days here, and then the dragon overtook me and cast me down. Just as I thought I would write you my enemy struck me in the right arm, so that I could not hold a pen or write a word. Moreover, I was unable to do or to think. Since then both feet have been imperial in colour, improper in proportions, and impotent for motion. This is now the third week of my sickness, but things are brighter. I can write, as you see, and I can walk across a room, and I can think, and I can trust, and not be afraid. Bless the Lord with me.

I pray that you may be preserved in all your goings. We have had the finest imaginable weather. Mr Alabaster leaves me to-morrow, and I expect Mr Passmore to-day.

Things seem quietly alive at home. I thank you much for remembering my dear wife, who toils and slaves while I luxuriate, or might do, if I were well.[1] That dear —— of yours, God bless him. May you both have a quiet, happy time. Go at half speed. Don't make camels and donkeys go like racehorses. I think of you both with loving gratitude, and would like to see you.

I try to go out a little ride, but it blows to-day, and so I shall be a prisoner. God is very gracious to me. I am now enrolled in the work-and-suffer corps, and expect to have double grace for the double part I am to sustain. Pray it may be so. Write again.

Yours ever most heartily,
C. H. SPURGEON

[1]On account of the nature of her own ill-health Susannah Spurgeon could seldom be with her husband at Menton.

Westwood
Beulah Hill
Upper Norwood
May 25, 1888

Dear Friend,

My dear wife is very very ill. To see any one is quite out of the question, she is confined to her bed. For myself I have been today devoid of any presentable teeth and twice at the dentist's, trying to get some teeth fitted that I may speak at my mother's grave tomorrow. Besides which I am ill and low.

To my great sorrow I find that your esteemed mother has been here to see Mrs Spurgeon.

My dear wife begs me to assure you that if she could have seen any one she would have seen your mother, but she must not see any one whatever. She hardly knows how close to death's gate she has been. It will be long before she can be well again.

All this is to explain why your good mother was disappointed. Of all the possible times it happened to be the most unfortunate and I beg her and you to excuse us. Indeed what could be done!

The Lord ever bless you.

Yours heartily,
C. H. SPURGEON

[*The Church at the Tabernacle*]

Westwood
Beulah Hill
Upper Norwood
[May] 1888

Dear Friends,

When I came home yesterday from my dear mother's grave I was lame. It was raw and cold, and my knee became painful, but I had no fear. About eight o'clock torrents of pain broke over me, and the knee was soon swollen. Now I cannot put the foot on the ground, and the pain is something to remember.

Please hear my dear friend, Mr Harrald, with thankfulness that at the eleventh hour he steps into the gap.

I send my love to you all, and great sorrow at being ill on a Sunday; but what can I do? The Lord make use of my great faggot of troubles for His own glory.

Yours sorrowfully,
C. H. SPURGEON

[*To be read at Prayer meeting*. Mr Frank Smith *will be there. Let him speak*]

Westwood
Beulah Hill
Upper Norwood
1888 Sabbath evening

Dear Friends,

As you love me pray for me specially just now. Never did I need your prayers more. Could you meet with one another to plead with God for me that I may be directed and sustained. The times are evil, and the trial for the man of God peculiar.

I am not well, but it will soon pass off and I hope speedily to be in full work. My teeth are troubling me just now, but if I once get over this, and my bodily weakness goes off I shall be up to the mark soon, by God's grace.

I am what and where I always have been in testimony to the truth. We shall as a church and people have to bear our witness for the Lord, and He will not fail us.

O that all of you may be aroused to pray, to bring the people in to hear the word, and to endeavour to win souls for Jesus. Again with deepest love to you I say 'pray'.

Your tired pastor,
C. H. SPURGEON

[*Rev Newman Hall*]

Menton
Jan. 20, 1889

Beloved Brother,

Your love allows brevity. Thank you. I am arising from stupor to pain, from pain to intervals of ease, from coughing hard to a weak voice, from writhing to wriggling about in an initial style of walking with a chair for a go-cart. I have had an escape which makes me shudder with gratitude. Here is a man who knocked out his teeth and yet did not cut his flesh, and turned over twice so completely as to put money into his boots. Something of the comic attends solemnity when I am in the midst of it. I have not lost a grain of peace or even of joy, yet I pity a dog that has felt so much in all his four legs as I have had in one.[1] All is well. I shall be home soon.

Yours most lovingly,
C. H. SPURGEON

[*Rev Dr D. A. Doudney*[2]]

Menton
Dec. 5, '90

Venerated Friend,

It made my heart leap for joy when I read in your note that you had liberty in prayer for me. I am recovering. I can hold the pen, as you see. My hand was puffed up, and, in consequence, like all puffed up things, useless; but it is coming to its true form, and I am rallying from the weakness which follows great pain.

Of a surety, it is well. I praise God with all my heart for the furnace, the hammer, and the file. May he bless to you the infirmities of years, and carry you ever in his bosom!

Your loving, grateful friend,
C. H. SPURGEON

[1]At Menton on the last Sunday of 1888 Spurgeon slipped and fell heavily on a marble floor. His first words to the alarmed friends who helped him up were on 'painless dentistry'! 'Neither pain nor weakness,' writes G. H. Pike, 'seemed to be able to repress the flow of his spirits or check his wit'.

[2]Anglican Editor of *The Gospel Magazine* and an old friend of Spurgeon's.

11: THE DOWN-GRADE CONTROVERSY

Nightingale Lane
Clapham
Dec. 29, 1877

Dear Friend,

I have been very ill and I have only now seen your letter, pray excuse delay but I have been kept from some things and I think rightly for my only illness is brain-weariness.

I don't know anything of Dowen's preaching. He has been to America and to my surprise has come back. There is nothing against him; but as he did not settle in England I have never spoken with any one who has heard him preach. The friends would soon know by trying him.

As to the other matter I am in deep perplexity and I am not in a condition of mind to lead. I feel deeply grieved at these utterances, and yet at the same moment the man is acting as only a great souled man could act. There are not above a dozen loose men among us to my knowledge, but an attack upon one might make a martyr of a party, and cause a world of trouble to the many faithful ones among us.

When I see my way I will move, but I do not at present. Do not let me hinder *you*. I shall have to be away for some time for I have been very ill, and I cannot now endure worry. Perhaps this weakness is on me for a purpose.

What do the Myrtle Street people say about all this? Does their church deed and trust allow such teaching? I fear that no parchments, no synods, no oaths even will keep men right: we must trust to the Spirit of God and betake ourselves to all prayer.[1]

Yours ever heartily,

C. H. SPURGEON

[*The Editor of* The Baptist]

Upper Norwood
May 27, 1881

Dear Sir,

If your leading article of this date had not been calculated to breed discord I should not have replied to it on my own account. From a remark as to the spiritual chill of the Union meetings, you infer a looseness of attachment to the Baptist Union, if not an intention to break away from it.[2] This is, indeed, a monstrous leap of logic. No one more heartily desires the prosperity of the Union than I do; no one is more satisfied with its designs and plans. If there be any mutterings of tempest they certainly do not arise from me or from any of those who gathered with me at the Conference.

It is a great pity that you so frequently abuse your

---

[1]This letter is significant as a forerunner of the far greater trouble with respect to biblical Christianity which became public ten years later in 'The Down-Grade Controversy'. See *The Full Harvest*, pp. 469–79, and *The Forgotten Spurgeon*, pp. 145–168.

[2]After the Baptist Union Conference of 1881 the denominational paper had published an article which referred to critics of the Union and mentioned the Tabernacle in particular. 'The Union is too cold for some perfervid spirits of that body'. Should these grumblers separate from the rest, the article went on to say, 'it is a moot question which of them would suffer most'. In the following seven years, as the letters which follow will reveal, there was to be a major change in Spurgeon's assessment of the state of the Union.

columns for the suggesting of discords. We are all, as far as I know, happily agreed, and if we venture to desire more fervency, or even leave the politics of the denomination to be managed by those who have a greater aptitude for such things, it is from no want of goodwill to the Union or to any part of it. You would do far more service if you imputed good motives whenever it was possible to do so.

Personally, I have shown my goodwill to the Union gatherings by very frequently speaking and preaching at them; and as I have declined to do this at the next autumn gathering, I should like it to be known that my sole and only motive is that I wish others to have their turn, and I would either absent myself or present myself, or do anything else to promote Christian love; but sometimes I am perplexed to know how to avoid giving offence in one way or another. Your paper has so much energy about it, and so much zeal for the growth of the denomination, that I feel sorry to see in it a sharpness which is not worthy of it. What can be the good of falling foul of your friends? At the same time, you are welcome to insinuate anything you please against me, if you will only believe that I am the hearty friend of the Baptist Union and all its works. How could I be otherwise? Everyone is much kinder to me than I deserve, and I dare say that even your disagreeable remarks are meant for my good.

> Yours very truly,
> C. H. SPURGEON

[*Dr S. H. Booth*]

Westwood
Beulah Hill
Upper Norwood
October 28, 1887

Dear Friend,

I beg to intimate to you, as the secretary of the Baptist Union, that I must withdraw from that society. I do this with the utmost regret; but I have no choice. The reasons are set forth in *The Sword and the Trowel* for November, and I trust you will excuse my repeating them here. I beg you not to send anyone to me to ask for reconsideration. I fear I have considered too long already; certainly every hour of the day impresses upon me the conviction that I am moving none too soon.

I wish also to add that no personal pique or ill-will has in the least degree operated upon me. I have personally received more respect than I desired. It is on the highest ground alone that I take this step, and you know that I have long delayed it because I hoped for better things.

Yours always heartily,
C. H. SPURGEON

Menton
November 23, 1887

Dear Mr Mackey,

As you are the scribe for the brethren, I thank you heartily, and beg you to let Mr Gracey and others know how cheered I am by the action of my beloved brethren.[1] I think the three resolutions most wise, as well as most loyal to the truth. I never desire my dear friends to follow me slavishly in every action, but to be influenced by that grand motive which I hope inspires me. Then there will be differences of operation, but all will work for one end.

It was encumbent upon me to leave the Union, as my private remonstrances to officials, and my repeated pointed appeals to the whole body, had been of no avail. My standpoint had become one from which, as an earnest man, I could see no other course but to withdraw. But you have made no such appeals, and might not be bound to do as I have done until you have had my experience of failure. That you will fail as I have done I fear; but you cannot do any harm by making an attempt. That you should march with me in a sympathy which is practically unanimous is a great consolation to my heart; for there are among our College confraternity two or three over whom I sorrow much. I will not think of them while I remember you, except it be to pray that they may return to their first love.

Let us daily pray for each other, in reference to the work which lies before us, that we may be faithful unto death – faithful not only to the doctrine of truth, but to the spirit of love – warring our warfare without trace of personal bitterness, but with stern resolve to spare none of the errors which insult the sacrifice of our Lord,

[1]Spurgeon had left London, on account of his poor health, early in November. On November 18 David Gracey (now Principal of the Pastors' College) had presided at a meeting of over a hundred Pastors' College ministers. Three resolutions had been passed. One of sympathy to Spurgeon and gratitude for the attitude he had taken. A second had reference to possible means to effect a return to the Union. A third decided that no action should be taken until after a report awaited from the Council of the Baptist Union.

destroy the way of salvation in this life, and then seek to delude men with the dream of salvation after death.

It is a great grief to me that hitherto many of our most honoured friends in the Baptist Union have, with strong determination, closed their eyes to serious divergences from truth. I doubt not that their motive has been in a measure laudable, for they desired to preserve peace, and hoped that errors, which they were forced to see, would be removed as their friends advanced in years and knowledge.

But at last even these will, I trust, discover that the new views are not the old truth in a better dress, but deadly errors with which we can have no fellowship. I regard full-grown 'modern thought' as a totally new cult, having no more relation to Christianity than the mist of the evening to the everlasting hills.

I desire my hearty love to each one of my true brothers in Christ, gratefully remembering in particular the learned chairman.

Yours most lovingly,
C. H. SPURGEON

Hôtel Beau Rivage,
Menton
Monday

Dear Mr Dunn,

I am free from pain. The weather is the perfection of delight. I am now getting real benefit. I have cast all care on Him who careth for us, and He will defend His own cause.

Distribute the 70 parcels of tea etc. to Almshouse women and then to the older poor members. Send blind

Mrs Watts a parcel. Let Brother *Parker* supply groceries to Almshouse as per usual.

I did not receive the Down Grade *Con*fession, but see it alluded to in British Weekly. I care little what is said. I know whom I have believed and what I have believed. Still it is a pity that even one in our church should lean to the wrong side.

I wrote Mrs Hale in answer to a kind letter from her.

I desire my hearty love to all the elders and helpers. God bless you.

Yours ever truly,
C. H. SPURGEON

Westwood
Beulah Hill
Upper Norwood
Feb. 8, 1888

Dear Joseph,

I have never doubted your *heart*, and I never even doubted the honesty of your head; but I feared you might get a little muddled. Still, I knew you were all right, true as steel. The Lord bless you for writing that note, for I am greatly cheered by it!

Samuel came up on Friday all at his own mind, and helped me. I think your town is a very hot-bed of New Theology fungi. Why do not the men avow it? You have been a great thorn in their side, and will be yet more so. The Lord will be with the truth.

I don't see quite what you can do yet, but there will be a time. They keep on clamouring for *names*. You can give me names. I don't want any one to be drawn in to personalities; but if they cry 'names', we shall have enough to give them.

Pray hard for me.

Yours heartily,
C. H. SPURGEON

Westwood
Beulah Hill
Upper Norwood
Feb. 15, 1888

Dear Friend,

I entreat your prayers, for I am heart-sore and weary with the desertions of those who should be at my side.

Nevertheless, the Lord will not fail me.

I am a poor creature for so great a battle. HE covereth my head, and yet I am ready to die. The Lord liveth, and therefore I have hope.

Yours heartily,
C. H. SPURGEON

Westwood
Beulah Hill
Upper Norwood
Feb. 21, 1888

Dear Friend,

The money came all right, and more. God be thanked! I am very grateful to *you*. Though I keep on continually, I cannot keep up letters.

I have been sorely wounded, and thought I should quite break down; but the Lord has revived me, and I shall yet see his truth victorious.

I cannot tell you by letter what I have endured in the desertion of my own men – Ah, me!

Yet the Lord liveth, and blessed be my Rock!

I am very grateful for your love. The Lord bless you for ever,

Yours heartily,

C. H. SPURGEON

Westwood
Beulah Hill
Upper Norwood
Feb. 21, 1888

Dear Friend,

Your letter was so loving and tender that it was 'as the small rain upon the tender herb.' God bless you for your loving sympathy!

I hope good will come of my warfare. It costs me dear. I thought last week I should die of grief. Still I live, yet not I.

Yours heartily,

C. H. SPURGEON

Westwood
Beulah Hill
Upper Norwood
Feb. 28, 1888

Dear Friends,

With all my heart I thank you. I have passed through a bitter season, but the Lord has sustained me, and now through the kind sympathy of His people He causes me to drink of the brook by the way and lift up my head.

Be constant in your prayers that by some means truth may prevail, and error may be put to shame. We are now in a very critical period, and only the bare arm of the Lord can bear us through all perils, and cause His church to come out of bondage.

I have more faith in the prayers of saints than in the wisdom of sages.

I am greatly cheered by the letters which are coming in from the churches.

The Lord has yet a people who abide by the truth.

Grace, mercy, and peace be with you all, pastor and people.

Yours gratefully,
C. H. SPURGEON

Westwood
Beulah Hill
Upper Norwood
April 27, 1888

Dear Mr Wright,[1]

I feel so ill, and so utterly crushed by last Monday[2] that I feel that I am only acting like a sensible man if I keep out of all Unions and Associations henceforth. I am over-burdened as it is with my own work, and this seems to indicate that I must not attempt more. If I began with your Association I should feel called upon to throw all energy into it and I have not the energy to spare. It would be looked upon as opposing the L.B.A.[3] from which I have withdrawn, and would involve me in a new controversy and secure me a grave. If we were dealing with men who receive language in its usual sense we might feel that very much was done on Monday, but I am not able to think so. We are sold; not betrayed but entrapped by diplomatists.

This note is for yourself only. I am very unwell. I don't feel that I can think much just now. My brother

[1]Possibly Mr G. Wright, pastor at Kingston and one of the leading men in the Pastors' College Association.

[2]The Baptist Union meeting in London on Monday, April 23, had passed by an overwhelming majority a resolution which it was supposed would end further controversy on any 'Down-Grade' in the Union. Spurgeon's concern that a fuller credal statement be adopted by churches in the Union was rejected and a report on the Council adopted which expressed the belief that there was no need of further tests 'of the evangelical character of the churches of the Union'. The main resolution was moved by Charles Williams (a liberal) and seconded by Spurgeon's own brother, Dr James Spurgeon. 'Those who acted', writes Pike, 'were complimented as striving after peace; but, as the sequel proved, the peace gained was not that abiding peace which many had anticipated' (*Life and Work of C. H. Spurgeon*), vol. 6, p. 302. See also *The Forgotten Spurgeon*, pp. 155–56).

[3]The London Baptist Association.

seems pleased with the idea of joining you, and I do not *altogether* abandon the idea, but do not say much about it or expect me at the meeting. Yours ever most heartily,

C. H. SPURGEON

Westwood
Beulah Hill
Upper Norwood
May 4, 1888

Dear Mr Wright,

I have definitely and finally resigned from the L.B.A. and shall not consider any further overtures to remain.

I am also resolved to join no body which is in union with the Baptist Union. In the case of your Association,[1] every man might be a personal member; but if the Association as such formed part of the Union, I had better not be invited to join.

The basis seems to me very good. Mr Greenwood should be asked too.

I fear that nothing whatever was gained on the 23rd but *words*, for all the modern men remain, and reckon themselves settled in their places.

I feel better now that my mind is made up never to return to a company so extremely clever in the use of language. I should never know what they meant, and like the good people at the Tower of Babel I should soon be on the move. I am happy with my dear faithful friends, and happier still with the God of truth.

Yours ever heartily,
C. H. SPURGEON

[1]This seems to be a reference to the Surrey and Middlesex Association; certainly it is not to the Pastors' College Association which had already been dissolved by Spurgeon and re-formed on a fresh theological basis.

Westwood
Beulah Hill
Upper Norwood
June 16, 1888

Dear Mr Near,

I do not see what else you can do. Are you in the Association? If so, you will still be in the Union. The Surrey, Middlesex, and Suburban is quitting the Union, and I shall probable [*sic*] unite with it. This will be an Association outside of the Union, sound in doctrine, and thus the nucleus of a fresh Union should the time come.

But there are many more rotten men in the Union than I dreamed of. The whole head is sick, and the whole heart faint.

I am not able to walk yet, but I shall try to preach on Sunday. I have my fears whether I can.

Yours ever heartily,
C. H. SPURGEON

Westwood
Beulah Hill,
Upper Norwood, S.E.
June 23, 1888

Dear Friend,

Keep to the Surrey and Middlesex which I hope to join. It will quit the Union. The more you have to deal with that evil Confederacy the worse you will like it. I am glad you have come out. I am not now quite alone.

Yours heartily,
C. H. SPURGEON

Westwood
Beulah Hill
Upper Norwood
Sept. 14, 1888

Dear Mr Wright,

I have hesitated about sending in an application till you are clear of the Union; and I don't want you to get clear for the sake of me. I am happier outside altogether, and I have no wish to join any Association, for I fear they will all sooner or later go wrong.

Still I shall send in an application to join with you when I know that I shall not thereby entangle myself with any Confederacy with evil.

Harrald is away and I cannot tell what day I can preach. Tuesdays are so full. Wednesday I could have managed more easily. I will do it if I can. He shall write.

Yours heartily,
C. H. SPURGEON

[*To the Ministers and Delegates forming the Baptist Convention of the Maritime Provinces of Canada*]

Upper Norwood
London
October 5, 1888

Dear Brethren in Christ,

I heartily thank you all for the words of cheer which you have sent me. Such a resolution, from such brethren, at such a time, gladdened me greatly. From the depths of my soul I thank all the brethren, and I pray the Lord richly to recompense them. I am grateful that you have not misjudged my action in reference to the English Baptist Union, from which I have felt bound to separate myself. I have not acted from sudden impulse, much less from any personal grievance; but I have been long protesting quietly, and have been at last compelled to make a stand in public. I saw the testimony of the churches becoming obscure, and I observed that in some instances the testimony from the pulpit was very wide of the Word of God, and I grieved over the state of things which is sure to follow upon defection from the Gospel. I hoped that the many faithful brethren would be aroused to the peril of the situation, and would earnestly endeavour to cleanse their Union of the most flagrant offenders. Instead of this, I am regarded as a troubler in Israel by many, and others feel that, important as truth may be, the preservation of the Union must be the first object of consideration. Nothing could have more fully proved to me that my protest is rather too late than too early.

On surveying the position, I perceive that the basis of our Baptist Union afforded nothing to work upon if a reform were attempted, for any person who has been immersed is eligible for membership. So far as anything found in the printed basis is concerned, every immersed person has a right to join it. Within its bounds there is neither orthodoxy nor heterodoxy, for all have an equal right of place. This does not appear to me to be the right condition of matters, and therefore I quitted the confederacy. Altogether apart from the soundness or unsoundness of individuals, the compact itself is on wrong grounds, and can never produce real unity. There are numbers of faithful, honoured, and beloved brethren in the Union; but these, by their presence and countenance, are bolstering up a confederacy which is upon a false foundation. It is not for me to censure them, any more than it was for them to censure me; but I cannot but feel that a more decided course of action on their part would have secured for our country a testimony to the truth which is greatly needed in these evil times; whereas their shielding of the false and erroneous has given a sanction to evil teachers which they are not slow to perceive.

The pain I have felt in this conflict I would not wish any other man to share; but I would bear ten thousand times as much with eagerness if I could see the faith once for all delivered to the saints placed in honour among the Baptist churches of Great Britain. I resolved to avoid personalities from the very beginning; and, though sorely tempted to publish all that I know, I have held my peace as to individuals, and thus have weakened my own hands in the conflict. Yet this also I had rather bear than allow contention for the faith to degenerate into a complication of personal quarrels. I am no man's enemy, but I am the enemy of all teaching which is contrary to the Word of the Lord, and I will be in no fellowship with it.

Nothing has occurred to cause my mind the least alienation from Baptist brethren who hold the doctrines taught in Holy Scripture. Far otherwise. I have never had a doubt as to the Scriptural correctness of our view of baptism; and I rejoice that with the mass of those who obey the Lord in this matter I am still in hearty union. Assuredly I am *one with you*, and all the more consciously so because you have not hesitated to stand by me in the hour of trouble, when many shun my company and condemn my conduct.

God bless you, my beloved brethren, and keep you in His faith as at this day! May the Lord increase and strengthen you more and more, and bless all the 'Maritime Provinces' through your works of faith and labours of love. You are not ashamed to state your beliefs. You do not wish to cover up error by a cloudy, indefinite state of things, which, like darkness, encourages evil. You love the truth, and therefore do not shun the light. May the Holy Ghost be with all your ministers, and dwell in all your members! Peace be to you and grace!

Unable to write all that I feel, I turn to prayer, and beseech our God in Christ Jesus to bless you exceeding abundantly above all that we ask or even think.

>Yours most gratefully, and lovingly,
>C. H. SPURGEON

>Westwood
>Beulah Hill
>Upper Norwood
>Nov. 16, 1888

Dear Friend,

Hearty thanks. In 'S. & T.'[1] for December I urge the necessity of separation. Alas, I speak to a deaf ear.

Yet our Lord lives, and His gospel is not altered.

Very, very weak, hope soon to move.

>Yours truly and lovingly,
>C. H. SPURGEON

>Westwood
>Beulah Hill
>Upper Norwood
>Feb. 20, 1890

Dear Mr Near,

Any brother who will sign the basis can return to our College Association, but I could not entertain any

---

[1] *The Sword and the Trowel*, produced monthly by Spurgeon from 1865.

proposal to make the signature optional. The Association is comprehensive enough in all conscience. I quite see with you that it is in some directions too much so; but I will sooner quit it finally than have any part of its doctrinal basis trifled with. I should not sympathise with any movement inviting those to return who left us, if it were made in the gross; but no one would be more glad than I to see brethren come back of their own accord, or to invite any who are apart from us through misunderstanding.

Yours very truly,

C. H. SPURGEON

Westwood
Beulah Hill
Upper Norwood
Feb. 22, 1890

Dear Mr Near,

Those who hold the fundamental truths can return to us[1] on the terms laid down, and on no others. If any other terms were proposed, I should simply end my connection with the matter.

I have suffered enough for one life time from those whom I had lived to serve. I will have no repetition of such an experience through any act of my own. Those who have gone from us can only expect to be treated as well as those who remained with us. If they are sincere believers they will be glad of the opportunity of declaring their faith.

Those who wish to return can come and welcome, and no one more pleased to see them than I; but not to doubtful disputations and cavillings.

[1] i.e., the Pastors' College Association.

I do not see why you should write of 'boycotting'. I have heard of nothing of the sort, and should condemn it. Yet, every man has a right to choose his own company.

> Yours ever heartily,
> C. H. SPURGEON

Every man signed the basis. To the best of my knowledge and belief there is no exception. Give me the names of any who did not.

12: LETTERS OF THE
LAST YEAR

1891 – 1892

[*William Olney*][1]

Menton
Jan. 31, '91

Dear Friend,

That Hastings incident raises my desire that we may see the like, God be praised. The old gospel is the real wonder-worker; the new stuff would not save a robin.

I am so glad you like the North Africa Mission. It is a live work *spiritually* – financially it needs *go*; but the spiritual element of faith in God delights me.

I have been in much bodily trial this week, but a dogged determination not to succumb has, by God's blessing, borne me onward, and I am getting on *now*.

Here I have souls won for Christ, but it is good mowing where there is much grass. Still 40 every morning is a pretty little congregation, and they are by no means ordinary folks, but people of education and thoughtfulness and influence. God bless you with sound health, and your dear mother also.

Yours heartily,
C. H. SPURGEON

[1]Son of William Olney who died in 1890 and, like his father and grandfather, one of Spurgeon's helpers and office-bearers.

[*Members of the Pastors' College Association*]

Metropolitan Tabernacle
Newington
S.E.
Mar. 10, 1891

My Dear Friend,

College Conference again! *O that the Lord would be in our midst this year in the fulness of his grace and power, and may we each one know it.* Come up to the feast if you can, and bring HIM with you, for our one great longing is to meet the King himself. John XI.56. Song I.12. II Chron. VII.1–3.

Being of one heart and of one soul, as I trust we are, we come together with one accord and wait for the one Spirit. HE will be the subject of our thoughts, and prayers, and the object of our praises, and we shall need his sacred aid that by his light we may see himself. I implore you to join with me in special private pleadings with God for a remarkable blessing. We cannot ask too much; but the buoyancy of faith must be equal to the weight of the request. We may set the measure of the blessing ourselves. Ps. LXXXI.10. Matt. VIII.13.

May you, dear brother, be a blessing to those who may entertain you. May our gatherings be a pleasant rest for you, and may the fellowship therein enjoyed brighten the gloom of toil and lighten the burden of service.

Do be so good as to answer our secretaries at once. It is really sad to see what needless trouble certain of our friends persist in causing us, when already the task of arranging such a gathering is by no means light.

Yours very lovingly,
C. H. SPURGEON

[*Office-Bearers at the Tabernacle*]

Westwood
Beulah Hill
Upper Norwood
April 27, 1891

Dear Friends,

The excessive strain of the week seemed suddenly to come upon me when I stood before the people on Sunday night. My mouth seemed to become dry so that my teeth would not keep their place, and my heart failed me with a fear of which I felt ashamed, but which I could not overcome. I have been so busy and so happy that I felt a sudden reaction and broke down. Don't be at all distressed about me. I shall soon be right. Indeed, I fancy I could preach *now*; but I must keep still this week, and be ready for next Sunday if the Lord will.

You will bear with me a little longer; and when I grow too old and feeble, you must find someone else.

Yours ever lovingly,
C. H. SPURGEON

Westwood
Beulah Hill,
Upper Norwood, S.E.
May 30, 1891

Dear Friend,

I have trembled on the edge of the abyss, and, now, though away from the crumbling sides I am weak as a little child.

Pray for

Yours truly,
C. H. SPURGEON

[*The Church at the Tabernacle*]

Menton
Dec. 24, 1891

My Dear Friends,

For the last time in the year 1891 I write you, and with this brief note I send hearty gratitude for your loving-kindness to me during the year which is ending, and fervent wishes for a special blessing on the year so soon to begin. I have nearly finished thirty-eight years of my ministry among you, and have completed XXXVII Volumes of published sermons, preached in your midst. Yet we are not wearied of each other. I shall hail the day when I may again speak with you. Surrounded by ten thousand mercies my time of weakness is rendered restful and happy; but still to be able, in health and vigour, to pursue the blissful path of useful service, would be my heaven below. To be denied activities which have become part of my nature, seems so strange; but as I cannot alter it, and as I am sure that infinite wisdom rules it, I bow before the divine will, – my Father's will.

Again the Doctor reports favourably. That is to say, yesterday he said that there was decided improvement as to the Disease: nothing great, but as much as he could hope for; – nothing speedy could be looked for, but matters were going most encouragingly. I was to be very careful about a chill, etc.

This is an old and dull story to you. Only your prayerful and persevering interest in me could make me bold enough to repeat it.

Honestly, I do *not* think you are losers by my absence, so long as the Lord enables our dear friend Dr Pierson to preach as he does. There is a cloud of blessing resting on you now. Turn the cloud into a shower by the heavenly electricity of believing prayer. May the Watch-night be a night to be remembered, and on the first hour of the year may the Lord say '*From this day will I bless you.*'

Yours with faithful love,

C. H. SPURGEON

[*The Church at the Tabernacle*]

Menton
Dec. 31, 1891

My Dear Friends,

I am sorry my letter of last week reached London too late for reading on Sunday, but this was occasioned by delays in the trains, and not by any omission on my part. It is kind on the part of so many newspapers to publish it, for thus I trust most of you have read it.

I believe I am right in reporting a greater change in the disease than could be spoken of before. It is still a great drain upon me; but as it has improved so far, I believe it will make more rapid diminution. What a joy it will be to be within measurable distance of the time to return to my pulpit and to you. I have not reached that point yet.

Now may the Lord cause the cloud of blessing to burst upon you in a great tropical shower. I am expecting this. Grateful beyond expression for all that the Lord has done and is doing, I am eager for more. Indulgence in covetousness is sinful, but not when we 'covet earnestly *the best gifts*'. All that I can do is to pray and expect. I am sometimes fearful lest anything in *me* should hinder the blessing; do you not each one feel the same fear on your own account? Before some sweet music is about to be heard there is a *hush*. Each one is afraid to breathe lest the tone should be spoiled and the music marred. I feel just so at this moment. May no whisper that would grieve the Holy Spirit be heard in house or heart. Let all coldness, worldliness, difference, or selfishness be put forth as the old leaven, that we may keep the feast of New Year without anything that defileth.

The Lord himself deal out to each one of his children a full portion, and to those who linger at the gate may the Good Spirit give his gracious drawings that they may cross the sacred threshold *this day*. Peace be within the gates of our dear sanctuary, and prosperity within her doors. For my brethren and companions' sake will I now say 'Peace be within thee'.

> Yours to serve when I can
> and to love unceasingly,
> C. H. SPURGEON

[*Rev Archibald G. Brown*]

> Menton
> January 2, 1892

Beloved Brother,

Receive the assurance of my heart-love, although you need no such assurance from me. You have long been most dear to me; but in your standing shoulder to shoulder with me in protest against deadly error we have become more than ever one. The Lord sustain, comfort, perfect you! Debtors to free and sovereign grace, we will together sing to our redeeming Lord, world without end.

> Yours most heartily,
> C. H. SPURGEON

To your faithful church the abiding presence of the Lord and the continued manifestation of His power.

[*The Church at the Tabernacle*]

Menton
Jan. 6, 1892

My dear Friends,

There is nothing for me to say in reporting myself to head-quarters beyond this – that I hope and believe that the steady and solid progress which had begun is continued, and will continue. If a doctor were to visit me now for the first time, and were to investigate my disease, he would pronounce it a bad case. But those who know what I have been, and how much worse than at present everything was – must wonder at me, and think it a remarkably good case. God be thanked for all that he has done in answer to his people's prayers. Never let us have a doubt as to the fidelity and ability of the God of the promises and of the mercy-seat.

On looking back upon the Valley of the Shadow of death through which I passed so short a time ago, I feel my mind grasping with firmer grip than ever that everlasting gospel which for so many years I have preached to you. We have not been deceived. Jesus does give rest to those who come to him, he does save those who trust him, he does photograph his image on those who learn of him. I hate the Christianised infidelity of the modern school more than ever, as I see how it rends away from sinful man his last and only hope. Cling to the gospel of forgiveness through the substitutionary sacrifice; *and spread it with all your might, each one of you,* for it is the only cure for bleeding hearts.

Peace be unto you as a whole; and peace be to each one! I greet with whole-hearted gratitude my brother Dr Pierson,[1] and with unfeigned love each deacon, elder, and member, and worker. My own dear brother in the flesh is also ever watching over the concerns of our great work. May the Lord himself keep watch over all. To Mr Stott I wish a long and prosperous ministry where the Lord shall direct him.

Yours ever lovingly,

C. H. SPURGEON

[*The Deacons, Metropolitan Tabernacle*]

Menton
1892

Beloved Brethren in Christ,

I know not how to express the wondering gratitude which continues to fill my mind and heart. That the Lord our God should hear the importunate prayers of His whole Church delights me, but does not surprise me. But that the Church should favour me with such a hearty and spontaneous outburst of loving solicitude, altogether amazes me. I am as one spared from the grave henceforth a double debtor to the people of God; and I can only acknowledge the debt, and seek to increase it by asking still to be remembered in prayer.

My recovery so far has been most remarkable. The cessation of the waste caused by the disease is very, very gradual; but as the case is altogether special, I expect, in answer to prayer, to receive a fuller cure than has been

---

[1]Dr A. T. Pierson, an American Presbyterian, was supplying the Tabernacle pulpit.

known aforetime. I desire this that I may, according to your desire, return to my public service, bearing witness to truth, wooing the souls that stray, and feeding the faithful of the flock.

I pray that to you, my brethren, the Lord may send a gracious recompense for your careful sympathy with me. From my inmost soul I thank you. Peace and prosperity be with all the churches of our Lord Jesus of every name and nation! May loving union prevail over all divergences of judgement, and may HE come, Who will be the consummation of our hopes!

> Yours with hearty gratitude,
> C. H. SPURGEON

[*Rev William Cuff*]

> Menton
> January 9, '92

My dear Mr Cuff,

I cannot write letters, but I can manage to sign a cheque. It is with much pleasure that I send you this £50, and I wish you might not have need of any more, though I see you will. Yours is a long task, and I wish I had a long purse with which to help you; but wishing will not bring it.

Doctor says I hold my own. In this broken weather it is all I can expect, and more.

I am truly grieved that you have so much family affliction. What fine clusters our Vine-dresser will get from so much pruning! Is it not a happy thing to live to see some of you, who were my young lads, becoming such truly great fathers in Israel, with your faithful churches around you?

I must think about Conference when I am better able to think of it. Suggestions can wait awhile.

God bless you!

Yours ever heartily,

C. H. SPURGEON

[*Joseph Passmore*]

Menton
Jan. 16, '92

My dear old Friend,

I have only good news to send you. I have not gone backward, but Doctor says I am a shade better as to my disease; in other respects, I feel up to the mark. Mrs S. well.

Beautiful ride half-way to Turbie this morning; turned back at the Fountain. Weather has been bad, but to-day is heavenly. Snow on the mountains just makes us the more grateful. Come along as soon as you can.

Mrs P. thanks you heartily, but does not know of anything which she desires.

I sent telegram of sympathy to Sandringham. I could not help it as the Prince had so kindly thought of me. May the Lord save all you love from this fell disease.

Yours ever lovingly,

C. H. SPURGEON

[*William Higgs*]

Menton
Jan. 20, 1892

My dear Friend,

The sun shines at length, and now I hope to get on. I have not been up to the mark the last few days, and I have a little gout in the right hand which makes it hard to write; but I shall soon get over it . . . I wired Prince of Wales, and had a telegram back, which I did not expect.[1] Shall be right glad to see you. Mrs S. is pretty well.

Yours very lovingly,
C. H. SPURGEON

The above words appear to have been the conclusion of all that Spurgeon wrote. They were read to the congregation at the Metropolitan Tabernacle on Sunday, January 24. But the hope they inspired was succeeded by a telegram telling of a serious relapse. The much-loved pastor and preacher died in the last hour of January at the age of fifty-seven. Close to the end he whispered to J. W. Harrald, 'Remember, a plain stone. C.H.S. and no more; no fuss.'

[1]Spurgeon had written to the Prince and Princess of Wales on the occasion of the death of their eldest son.

INDEX

In this Index the abbreviations CHS, MT and NPSC are used for C. H. Spurgeon, Metropolitan Tabernacle and New Park Street Chapel.

SOME OTHER
SPURGEON TITLES

THE FORGOTTEN SPURGEON
Iain Murray

This book traces the main lines of Spurgeon's spiritual thought in connection with the three great controversies in his ministry – the first was his stand against the diluted Gospel fashionable in the London to which the young preacher came in the 1850's; the second, the famous 'Baptismal Regeneration' debate of 1864; lastly, the lacerating Down-Grade controversy of 1887 – 1891 when Spurgeon sought to awaken Christians to the danger of the Church 'being buried beneath the boiling mud-showers of modern heresy'.

ISBN 0 85151 156 2
264pp. Paperback. Illustrated.

SPURGEON: A New Biography
Arnold Dallimore

It is fitting that Dr Arnold Dallimore, author of a two-volume *Life of George Whitefield* (and more recently of a *Life of Edward Irving*) should now give us a book on Charles Haddon Spurgeon (1834–92). This is a concise narrative of Spurgeon's life. He has set out 'to understand and present something of the inner man – Spurgeon in his praying, his sufferings and depressions, his weaknesses and strengths; in his triumphs, humour, joys, and incredible accomplishments'.

It is no easy task to depict 'so tremendous a personality' as that of Spurgeon in a brief volume, but in 272 pages it is here accomplished, and with a large measure of success. It will meet the need of those completely ignorant of Spurgeon and his vast achievements, but will stir also the interest of all who value a unique ministry, yielding 62 volumes of 'deathless' sermons and many other highly valuable publications.

ISBN 0 85151 451 0
272pp. Large Paperback. Illustrated.

METROPOLITAN TABERNACLE
PULPIT Volume 38 (1892)

C. H. Spurgeon

In the sixty-two annual volumes of *The Metropolitan Tabernacle Pulpit*, possibly the most remarkable publishing venture in the history of the Christian church, the present volume for the year 1892 was numbered 38. While no different in many respects from the other volumes in the series, it must have special appeal to all who value Spurgeon's writings. Leading these fifty-two sermons (exactly half from the Old Testament) are the last which he personally prepared for the press before his death at the age of fifty-seven on January 31, 1892. His last letters, printed with the sermons, give them special poignancy.

ISBN 0 85151 611 4

640pp. Cloth-bound.

C. H. SPURGEON:
AUTOBIOGRAPHY

Volume 1: The Early Years, 1834–1860
Volume 2: The Full Harvest, 1861–1892

The story of Spurgeon's life, largely in his own words, from the events of childhood and youth until the years of his ministry in New Park Street (Volume 1); and then through the period of his mature ministry when twice each Sunday he preached to a capacity congregation of 6,000 people at the Metropolitan Tabernacle. Here is an inspiring record of a Christian life which continues to be of blessing for so many.

Vol. 1 ISBN 0 85151 076 0   *580pp. Cloth-bound. Illustrated.*

Vol 2. ISBN 0 85151 182 1   *536pp. Cloth-bound. Illustrated.*

THE LIFE AND WORK OF
C. H. SPURGEON

G. Holden Pike

From the earliest days of his ministry Spurgeon's work was many-sided. It was characterized by an enduring commitment to Scripture and a Calvinistic theology of grace. In every sense his was a large life, lived enthusiastically for the glory of Christ.

Of the many biographies of Spurgeon, this by G. Holden Pike is of special interest. First published in 1894, two years after Spurgeon's death, it gives an account of his life by one who, for thirty years, observed him at close quarters and knew him intimately.

ISBN 0 85151 622 X

2-volume set, 608pp. per volume
Cloth-bound. Illustrated.

AN ALL-ROUND MINISTRY

One of Spurgeon's greatest ministries was to the hundreds of preachers who were trained in the Pastors' College he founded. In 1865 he began an annual conference for them, and during his life delivered 27 Presidential Addresses. The very best of them are contained in this convenient paperback.

ISBN 0 85151 181 3

416pp. Paperback.

For free illustrated catalogue please write to:
THE BANNER OF TRUTH TRUST
3 Murrayfield Road, Edinburgh EH12 6EL
P.O. Box 621, Carlisle, Pennsylvania, 17013, U.S.A.